1998

MAKING PEACE AT MAYFIELD

MAKING PEACE AT MAYFIELD

A Whole School Approach to Behavior Management

Colleen Breheney, Vicki Mackrill and Neville Grady

Heinemann
Portsmouth, NH

Heinemann
A Division of Reed Elsevier Inc.
361 Hanover Street
Portsmouth, NH 03801-3912

Offices and agents throughout the world

ISBN 0 435 07229 3
Published simultaneously in the United States
in 1996 by Heinemann
and in Australia by
Eleanor Curtain Publishing
906 Malvern Road
Armadale, Australia 3143

Production by Island Graphics
Edited by Ruth Siems
Text and cover design by David Constable
Typeset in 11/14 Garamond by Island Graphics
Cover photograph by Carol Davidson
Printed in Australia

Foreword

T HIS IS A BOOK of hope. It is about a school that decided to make a difference in a demanding and difficult social environment. There are many critics of education and schools these days – too many. Against much that is ill-informed, this book shows how schools can significantly affect a community.

The 'client-group' (students and parents) presented a demanding challenge to the school. However, the school refused to accept this 'dark-side' or to fall into a state of resignation and siege mentality ('What can you really expect from *these* kids ...!'; 'No wonder they can't learn ...'; 'Is it worth it ...?'; 'Nothing we do matters ...'; 'What these kids need is a good kick up ...').

We can't easily, directly, change many of the factors that work against the positive development of children: parental attitudes, values and norms, discipline patterns at home, attitudes to education and schooling. Many of those factors are unalterable from the school; but we can change the environment they come into. *Our* school. How can we make this place a place to belong, to feel safe, to enjoy and learn respect, to learn, to grow ...? Let's work on that environment and bring to it our effort, energy and skill.

This school has done something about an environment where hostility, suspicion, poor communication and conflict, even violence, were a daily pattern. It wasn't easy. The staff, under visionary, committed and practical leadership *decided* to make a difference. What they did – their journey – is the substance of this book.

It didn't just happen. In turning the school around, a team effort had to come to terms with what its community was and what they could do to build a positive ethos, climate and learning environment. They addressed a wide range of issues affecting curriculum, teaching and learning styles, physical layout and environment, the way they encouraged and celebrated individual and group success, and, most of all, how they could enable students to manage their behavior in a positive, non-violent way. A tall order.

The book is the story of one school's journey. The authors do not claim to provide a blueprint for all schools, but there is ample here in precept, principle and practice that any school could not only learn from but translate to their situation.

It shows how a whole-school approach can and does work when staff have vision, good will, skills and determination to 'hang in there' for the benefit of children.

Schools can never be a substitute for a loving, supportive, secure family environment able to cope with the inevitable tensions of daily living. They *can*, however, provide a place where children are valued, believed in and treated as worthwhile. Children spend a third of their waking day at school. For some, 'that place' may be the sanest, most consistent, just and secure place in their uneasy lives.

I warmly encourage you to read this book. It is a book for all staff, all schools. I commend my colleagues for their commitment, good will and courage in the face of significant stress and difficulty – they have made a difference in the lives of 'their' children.

Bill Rogers

Contents

Acknowledgments

We wish to thank the following people for their invaluable support in the writing of this book:

The acting principal, Kelly Heathcote, and staff of Mayfield Primary School, and, in particular, Peter Claridge, Maree Duggan and Louise Fisher for their assistance in the writing of chapter 3.

The children of Mayfield who expressed honest and valuable opinions on the past and present climate of the school.

The parents whose pride, commitment and hard work encouraged us to see the project through.

Carol Davidson for her expertise with her camera and Jane Tobin who did valuable work in finalising the script.

Elizabeth Daly, district superintendent, for her formal and informal encouragement.

Bill Rogers for being our mentor and friend.

Preface

Books about schools generally adopt a particular focus or perspective, and this one is no exception. It illustrates one school's experience as it addressed the nature of its children's behaviors, especially inappropriate ones such as fighting. That such a focus is timely is evidenced by regular media articles presenting details of violent episodes in schools and by a range of government inquiries.

Over the past two years, counsellors, consultants, teachers, and others interested in this subject have sought details of Mayfield Primary School's approach. To date, such requests have been satisfied by providing various bits and pieces of documented material, and this book is our attempt to bring that material together in a coherent fashion and to provide some background to its rationale.

The content is organised into three chapters.

Chapter 1 describes the school as it was several years ago when behaviors throughout the school and the welfare of the children within the school were of serious concern – the dark side. It discusses indicators of school effectiveness, and goes on to describe Mayfield as it is today – the bright side.

Chapter 2 represents our attempt to describe how Mayfield turned the dark side slowly around to reveal its bright side, and to describe the major forces and processes for change.

Chapter 3 describes the various programs that were developed at Mayfield to minimise violence and to promote appropriate behaviors. These programs are of a whole-school and classroom-based nature and provide the reader with practical teaching and organisational strategies for developing positive behaviors.

Colleen Breheney and Vicki Mackrill were principal and senior teacher respectively during this time, and were intimately involved in the change process. It is never easy to analyse complex, emotional and ambiguous situations in which one is a central player. Nevertheless, we hope that we have been able to paint a useful picture of the process.

We have identified four major areas which we regard as being central to the change:

- leadership towards a shared vision
- leadership through an organisational culture characterised by rights and responsibilities
- improvement through a focus on professional and curriculum development
- improvement through parent education and participation

We conclude with a claim that success was due essentially to people demonstrating the 6 Cs: Concern, Commitment, Cohesion, Collaboration, Coping skills and a capacity for Celebration.

Towards effectiveness

1

THIS BOOK REPRESENTS a celebration of one school's success in moving to a state of relative effectiveness in the teaching of positive behaviors, and sets out to explain how that success was achieved.

Mayfield Primary, a school of 250 children from Kindergarten to Year 6, is situated in one of Launceston's oldest state housing areas. Many children have learned behaviors judged by the principal and teachers, at least, to be inappropriate. The limited facilities at hand locally, poor transport to and from the area, and the lack of money in the family purse mean that many children have few opportunities to experience the world beyond their local community and to witness alternative behaviors.

The dark side

Early in 1990, not long after Colleen Breheney took up the principalship of the school, she observed a large number of children exhibiting inappropriate behaviors, some of which were excessively violent. Indeed, Breheney saw that violence was endemic throughout the school: in the playground, in the classrooms, in the corridors, in the toilets.

> I had worked for nine years before to being appointed to Mayfield, in what I believed were similar schools to this. I did not expect any surprises or cultural shocks.
>
> Although there were similarities with other schools, I was not really prepared for the degree or extent of the violence at Mayfield. There seemed to be so many sad, angry people, full of despair.
>
> I remember in that first week walking around the playground at lunchtime watching and intervening in many violent incidents and 'thinking this place is out of control'. I rang the bell early that day because I was in fear of something really dreadful happening. It was the only short-term strategy I could think of at that time.
> – Colleen Breheney

Breheney and other senior staff documented examples of this behavior in files of individual children and in their own journals. A small sample of these entries illustrates the situation at the time.

A Year 2 girl ran home after a fight in her classroom; her ear was cut, her hand was bitten, and her face was scratched

Before school, a large group of Year 3 boys left their classroom in Block A, entered a Year 2/3 classroom in Block B and began pushing and grabbing, kicking and hitting children in this class.

A Year 5 boy walked into the time-out area which was being supervised by the principal. In a cold and callous manner, he strolled past the principal, who thought he had been sent from the playground, and viciously kicked in the head a boy who was sitting on the floor.

A fight broke out between two 11-year-old boys in the playground over an incident that happened at the weekend. After one child was punched to the ground, the other proceeded to kick him in the head before the supervising teacher could intervene.

A Year 6 girl was not permitted into the playground because of previous vicious attacks she had made on small children. She frequently kicked and punched them to the ground, and generally acted as a 'terrorist'.

A Year 3 girl, after refusing to work in class, yelled abuse, left the room and returned with a steel grate which she threw across the classroom in a rage.

A group of 5-year-old boys cornered a 5-year-old girl in a covered entrance way and proceeded to 'mock' rape her.

A Year 5 boy threw a can of Coca Cola at another Year 5 boy, hitting him on the head. He then punched him. A teachers' aide and a teacher intervened and were punched. The boy was eventually restrained by two teachers and taken inside to an office. The saga continued there with the police ultimately being called.

Two boys from the same family were rarely permitted into the playground because of the head-high kicks they often administered to victims.

A Year 5 boy was brought to the principal's office following a day of truancy. He was asked to discuss the matter with her but he attempted to leave, and when stopped at the door he turned quickly and punched his hand through a window.

A Year 6 boy was teased by a Year 5 girl in class. A teacher intervened as the boy attempted to stab the girl with scissors.

Criminal offences by children both at school and in the larger community are a major problem. A 7-year-old was found asleep on top of the monkey bars, having broken into the local football club and stolen alcohol the night before. He and his older mates had been 'partying' all night.

Some parents also exhibited violent behavior towards their own children, and to other members of the school community. This was also documented.

A parent stormed into a classroom wielding a leather belt and demanding to beat her child in front of the class to teach him a lesson.

A highly intoxicated parent arrived unannounced at a classroom accusing the teacher of locking her child in a room. The parent threatened the teacher physically before dragging her child from the class.

A fight broke out between two feuding male parents outside a classroom where they and other parents were waiting to pick up children at the conclusion of the day.

The police had to be asked to attend the school fair because of the neighborhood feuding involving some parents.

The staff demonstrated a limited range of strategies to cope with these behaviors, and suspensions of children from school were a regular occurrence. It is not surprising that teachers generally exhibited high levels of stress. Examples of teacher behavior which reflected this stress included:

- displaying shallow coping skills in regard to behavior management, e.g. shouting at and manhandling children
- being absent from school frequently
- crying and offering other emotional displays
- rushing and appearing frantic
- indicating tiredness and exhibiting little energy or enthusiasm
- fearing failure and believing that something would go wrong in their classes each day

- trying to survive rather than being able to put into effect sound teaching and learning programs
- being angry and negative towards children and the school
- blaming others
- playing the victim
- having low expectations in regard to children's behavior and academic success

> I only used to go to the toilet with Jarrod 'cause you'd get bashed up if you went by yourself.
> – Greg, Year 2

- requesting transfers to other schools

Others in the community, similarly, demonstrated a limited range of appropriate strategies to handle their anger and frustration. Outcomes included vandalism of the school, particularly the daily breaking of windows, and teachers' cars in the carpark being scratched.

Mayfield Primary School

Indicators of effectiveness

It is clear that some schools are more successful than others. Reid, Hopkins and Holly (1987; 4), for example, explained this claim as follows:

> At the end of my very first day teaching (if teaching is what it could be called) a class of Year 2/3 children at Mayfield Primary, I was sitting in my chair with most of the children 'sort of' sitting in front of me in a very disorganised way, with at least one large Year 3 boy sitting under a table at the back of the room refusing to come anywhere near the rest of the group and telling anyone who went near him to 'piss off', and I felt compelled to say to the children, that I felt that they had treated me like something 'less than human' during the day. One of the more difficult children then looked at me with a glint in his eyes from under his skinhead haircut and responded, 'You mean like a dog?', and then proceeded to laugh and to roll backwards into a somersault kicking other children in the back as he went.
>
> At that moment the siren thankfully sounded, the room became quickly deserted, and I collected my things and walked down to my office. I was sitting at my desk staring at the photographs of my cats when Colleen poked her head tentatively around my office door and said, 'How did it go?', to which I promptly burst into tears. She immediately came over and gave me a big hug, which was a great comfort, as her expectation that perhaps my day might be something other than easy made me realise that perhaps it was not necessarily a fault of mine that the day was so rotten!
> – Staff member

. . . two pupils from outwardly similar backgrounds and with similar intellectual abilities can perform differently at two outwardly similar schools because of the unique blend of academic and social circumstances to be found within the two establishments.

Here we attempt to explain how those academic and social circumstances were moulded over a three- or four-year period at Mayfield Primary School. We do not suggest that a 'recipe' for success for all schools, or for any other particular school, will be found here. Any attempt to search for a single solution would deny the contextual realities of schools: the socioeconomic background of the students and of their environment more generally, the degree of parental support for what the school is trying to do, the legal framework, the political scene, and systemic policies. Nevertheless, we believe that experiences of people in schools that have been able to enjoy some success within their particular context – whether at Mayfield or anywhere else – can provide valuable guidance for others who are contemplating their journey into the future.

Similarly, we do not espouse a single refined theory or set of theories concerning effectiveness, because, in keeping with the advice of Holdoway and Johnson (1993; 186), we believe that:

> . . . theories of effectiveness will change as we learn more about the components of effectiveness and our view of the components will change as our conception of effectiveness is modified. Such an iterative process is needed in educational research generally, and in school effectiveness research in particular; early closure is to be resisted.

What is certain though is that schools are complex tapestries, and it is foolish to suggest that a single aspect of these tapestries – say student performance on standardised tests in reading and numeracy – can provide even a rough rule-of-thumb measure of how effective any school is.

We believe that any worthwhile and sensible view of school effectiveness must be a multifaceted view. Sets of dimensions such as goal attainment, adaptability, satisfaction and commitment to life-long learning should be the focus. Furthermore, time scales being considered should range from short-term to long-term; the individual, class groups, and the whole school ought be regarded as important; and the perspectives of a variety of stake holders, including students, teachers and parents, must be given due regard (see, for example, Hoy & Miskel 1987).

Chapman (1993) uses the 'school as rope' metaphor to explain this multifaceted nature of schools. In one long piece of rope, no single fibre runs the entire length and no distinct fibres run from each end to meet in the middle; instead, a rope is a complex interweaving of many small, separate, overlapping fibres. So school effectiveness, said Chapman, should not be seen in terms of single definable entities. Instead it should be understood as:

> . . . complex interwoven layers of fact-and-value, descriptions-evaluations, framed in the context – bathed in the light, so to speak – of the institutions and contexts that give such words, concepts and conceptual networks meaning, purpose and applicability (p. 5).

Effective schools, in other words, are more than the sum of a number of dimensions and are achieved through processes beyond the mere pursuit of markers or indicators relevant to those dimensions. For example, even if a school gains parent and district support, recognises academic success, ensures that students spend a high proportion of time on academic activities, and puts in place a set of rules aimed at promoting an orderly environment, effectiveness will not necessarily result. Despite this, it is useful to know what some of these individual dimensions and particular processes are.

One of the most helpful early American reviews of the literature about effective schools was provided by Purkey and Smith (1983). They listed a number of variables which suggest effectiveness in two broad groupings:

organisational or structure variables, such as:

school-based management

instructional leadership

staff stability

goal consensus

school-wide staff development

parental and district support

school-wide recognition of academic success

maximum use of learning time

process variables, including:

collaborative planning and collegial relationships

organisational commitment

clear goals

high expectations

well-developed rules which underpin an orderly working environment

Useful Australian reviews include those by Mulford (1986) and Caldwell and Spinks (1986). The latter lists 43 characteristics of highly effective schools under six broad headings:

curriculum

decision-making

resources

outcomes

leadership

climate

As part of its ongoing evaluation of whole-school effectiveness, Mayfield employs a wide range of indicators which it judges to be relevant to its purposes and processes.(These indicators were developed at the end of the second year.) This is a formal and collaborative process, usually undertaken during whole-staff professional development time, where teachers work together to brainstorm those features they feel best indicate an improvement in the school. This process is viewed within both a short-term and long-term context using ongoing documented evidence as well as subjective impressions from all members of the school community. These indicators are:

School in general

having a quiet, calm atmosphere

offering a good variety of programs

demonstrating good management of time and other resources

being of good appearance

having a shared focus among teachers, children and parents

enjoying adequate resources

attracting sponsorship and support for the school

Children

having greater desire to learn

solving their own problems

paying each other compliments

working collaboratively

accepting consequences more readily and charitably

taking responsibility for each other

initiating own learning/interest development

demonstrating mutual respect for each other and for staff

appearing more confident in conflict situations

demonstrating less vandalism and more respect for common areas

understanding and respecting reasonable expectations placed upon them

having pride in school and in themselves

Parents

choosing to keep children in the school

desiring to send children to this school because of positive reports

increasing their involvement at school

complaining less frequently

providing positive feedback

encountering fewer problems between families in school-related matters

increasing confidence in, and ownership of, the school

maintaining eye contact with teachers

taking an active part in their children's education

demonstrating concern for teachers

adopting aspects of the school's mode of operation at home

Staff

having low absenteeism

having high morale

supporting each other

demonstrating respect for others' opinions

appreciating that duty is not such an onerous task

valuing the excellent cleaners and groundstaff

engaging in ongoing professional development

promoting a common philosophy with the neighboring secondary school

While it is sensible to view schooling as being multidimensional, we warn against the pursuit of impossible all-embracing goals such as the 'whole education of the whole child'. No school, regardless of how well resourced or governed it may be, can or ought to attempt to do everything. Nevertheless, we agree with Banks' claim, when reporting on the Effective Schools Project in which she was involved, that there is an essentially Australian view of what constitutes an effective school, and '... the strong message that emerges is that Australian school communities value the social and emotional well-being and development of students as well as their intellectual development.' (1992: 17). It is unlikely that these sentiments are confined to Australia.

Banks identifies several '... essential areas in which teachers could begin to concentrate their energies – and maybe gather new skills – if the community accepts that schools have a new and critical role to play in keeping our world viable [in the face of an imperative for peace in an environment that obviates it].' (1994; 6)

The first of these essential areas, according to Banks, is that schools must be safe places for all children, where mutual respect and good interpersonal relationships within the entire school community exist, where physical punishment is banned, and where consistent and fair non-violent solutions to inappropriate behavior are practised. We endorse Banks' claims fully, and believe that such thoughts actually underpinned our actions from the outset.

Mayfield Primary School's journey from what might be described as the 'dark side', even though it was begun well before Banks' words saw the light of day, was guided by a powerful, unshakable commitment by an ever-increasing number of people to these elements. Put another way, it was held that Mayfield could become a place which:

• is safe for all children (and others)

• functions on the basis of mutual respect and good interpersonal relationships

• practises consistent and fair non-violent solutions to inappropriate behavior

In line with Banks' plea for schools to be safe places, Breheney believed that no place, school or anywhere else, should be like the dark side of Mayfield. Also, Breheney support the belief that:

> Schools are not buildings, curriculums and machines. Schools are relationships among people. It is the interaction patterns among people, among students, between students and teachers, among teachers, between teachers and administrators, and among administrators that determine how effective schools are. (Johnson & Johnson 1989; 101)

Without a safe environment and good relationships, no school programs can be effective, regardless of the nature of the outcomes at which they are pitched. Children cannot learn bat and ball skills, or become independent readers, or work cooperatively in a group if the environment in which they are operating is unsafe, threatening, violent, unpredictable, or characterised by poor interpersonal relationships.

In short, Mayfield, while in its era of darkness, did not satisfy many of these indicators and, therefore, did not exhibit the prerequisites deemed to be essential for effective teaching and learning.

The bright side

Four years on, Mayfield satisfies a broad suite of effectiveness tests in far greater measure than it did before. This claim is illustrated by the following testaments from a variety of people, and by other tangible evidence.

Gaye is a very experienced teacher who currently spends her time in several schools each week, including one-and-a-half days at Mayfield. Six weeks into her first term at Mayfield, Gaye said to Mackrill, who was acting principal at this stage:

> I love working in this school. I find it a warm and welcoming place. I feel that friendliness, care, cooperation, and support pervade the school. I have easy access to information from individual staff. I find the school documents relevant and well prepared and it seems that they are reviewed and updated regularly. The relationships between all members of the school community are positive. There is respect and support for everybody and everything.
>
> I feel that there is quality leadership and support. The staff are committed and are professional in all aspects of the school's programs.
>
> The physical environment is well kept, spotlessly clean and attractive. The school is well equipped with teaching and learning materials and the management of these materials is fair and highly organised.

Monique is a district special education resource teacher who comes to the school one day a fortnight. Monique offered the following comments:

> Mayfield is one of the best schools in which I work. I am made to feel very welcome. Staff interact with me in a relaxed and friendly manner. The teachers and the teachers' aides speak positively about the children in the school and genuinely believe that children will achieve.
>
> All members of staff are supportive of one another, and offer advice and help concerning the children. I observe teachers working together

as a team to solve problems and to manage conflict. Programs within the school are very well organised and routines are in place which give children guidelines about behavior, teacher expectations and academic work. I witness social skills being taught to children in a formal way, and, even more importantly, I observe the children practising these skills over and over again in their interactions with other children and adults.

Leonie, the administrative officer, is the first face I see when I come to the school. She welcomes me in a warm and authentic manner, and this attitude extends throughout the school.

A small group of experienced educators from South-East Asia visited the school recently and offered the following statement:

We were met in the car park by two bright-eyed girls from Year 6. Vanessa and Belinda escorted us to the principal's office where they introduced us to Kelly [the principal] and one of her senior teachers, Peter. Significantly, Vanessa and Belinda (who both indicated that they wanted to be doctors later in their lives) stayed with us for much of our time in the school (including our time in Kelly's office and in the staff room at morning tea time) and explained things to us as we toured the classrooms and the school generally.

Kelly's office is a very welcoming place. Her desk and chair are located to one side, while the major part of the room is occupied by comfortable chairs, a coffee table and children's furniture and soft toys. Kelly's guitar stands in one corner so that it easily accessible if she is required to take over a class without notice.

As Peter outlined what he had arranged for us it was clear that he was enthusiastic about the school and its programs and students.

The seven of us, together with our escort from the university, saw many examples of students learning and practising appropriate behaviors in class meetings, in their normal classroom interactions and in their various programs. It was interesting to see how well the children were able to communicate their experiences to their peers and to offer suggestions as to how they might act when, for example, they were being bullied or belittled by others. At times, as we moved from room to room, children invited us to see their work and to work with them, but one of the most memorable moments occurred when two Year 5 boys, quite unrehearsed and spontaneously it seemed, quietly thanked us as we were leaving the room for visiting their class.

In the playground, we watched for a considerable time as a Year 6 boy coached, managed, played and umpired a basketball game involving boys and girls of different ages, sizes and skills. He undertook these tasks with great enthusiasm and expertise. Here was, we thought, a great leader at work. He was self-assured and knowledgeable and the other children gladly accepted his guidance and decisions. In some ways this boy was operating at a level which few teachers could exceed or, indeed, match. Other children led groups in various parts of the playground, while an adult joined boys and girls in a complex football game. Those children who weren't involved in organised activities seemed to be absorbed in various games such as marbles or played on monkey bars and the like.

> In the first year that my child was at Mayfield she often came home talking about the fighting and the bad behavior in the playground and the classrooms, and I thought I should pull her out and send her to the school down the road. I spoke to Colleen about my concerns and fears, and was made to feel as if things would get better, and that I could help in making things better for not only my child but perhaps some others in the school, through working together. — Parent

Two boys, it seemed, had behaved inappropriately, and were sent to a time-out seat. One accepted this graciously and negotiated a penalty with the duty teacher. The other was not prepared to carry out his part of a previously negotiated solution: 'It's not my job to pick up rubbish; cleaners are paid to do that,' he explained somewhat sullenly. The duty teacher went through a customary routine calmly, but to no avail, so the boy was sent to time-out inside the building.

At the end of the lunch break, the Year 3–6 students assembled in lines. Peter 'took charge', but this was no military camp. Good humor was evidenced as punctuality and tidiness were recognised, as class groups made and announced decisions, and as some general messages were delivered.

From what we saw in our four hours in the school, Mayfield is a fine school – at least as good as the best in our own country.

This chapter has attempted to paint a picture of two sides of the one school separated by about four years in time and by a world of difference in providing a foundation for good quality teaching and learning to occur. Mayfield moved some way to addressing Diana Banks' plea: 'Global survival will depend on cooperation at all levels of the community, from the local to the international, and I do not believe that children who grow up with violence will suddenly start using cooperative means to solve problems when they become adults. As an educator, I want my profession and the rest of the community to take this trend seriously and deal with it, not ignore it.' (Tasmanian Primary Principals Conference, Shearwater, 1993

The forces for improvement at Mayfield

2

W<small>E HAVE DRAWN</small> on our recollections of literature that provides guidance on school improvement matters – sometimes consciously, but, we suppose, sometimes unconsciously – to help us to organise our thoughts. We are particularly indebted to some of the work done by Matthew Miles and his colleagues, and especially to the guidelines provided in one of Miles' (1987) papers. The structure and details of this chapter reveal the influence of Miles' 'map' of relationships (often in what is claimed to be of a causal nature) which seem to be evident in schools that have successfully institutionalised quality programs. Nevertheless, our work here ought not be viewed, necessarily, as any sort of test of the adequacy or otherwise of this 'map'.

The major aspects of Mayfield's change experience can be described as the development and adoption of a shared vision, the promotion of an organisational culture which pays respect to personal rights and responsibilities, professional and curriculum development, and parent education and participation.

At the heart of this four-pronged strategy is a cooperative model akin to that described by Stevens and Slavin (1995). The model includes elements such as widespread use of cooperative learning methods in classrooms, teachers coaching each other and collaborating in instructional planning, principal and teachers collaborating on school planning and decision-making, and teachers and principal encouraging active involvement of parents. It provides a powerful foundation for the development and implementation of a number of programs at the classroom and playground level.

Leadership towards a shared vision

Mayfield's success in creating an environment of relative safety, calm, good relationships and productivity is due largely to the set of programs (described in chapter 3) which now operate throughout the school. Such programs must 'fit' the students, the parents, the staff, the neighborhood, and district office personnel, but, even more importantly, they must be romanced, developed, adapted, trialled, monitored, reworked and played with by dedicated, enthusiastic and competent staff. In order to do this, staff need to be led to identify and pursue a common goal.

FROM A PERSONAL VISION TO A SHARED VISION

It is fair to say that Breheney was driven initially by a personal vision for Mayfield Primary.

Sheive and Schoenheit (1987) held that just as pearls begin with an irritant within an oyster's shell, so too one's universal or organisational vision may begin with an irritation. Breheney's irritant presented itself on the first day of her appointment to the school and it festered over the next day or so to form a deeply held belief concerning two school matters. The first was that relationships between children in the school, surely, need not be as bad as they revealed themselves to be. The second was a concern that many children in the school were deeply unhappy, and that this should not be the case.

> At that first staff meeting I remember looking around at the very committed professional staff that were seated with me. I opened the meeting by saying that I believed it was obvious that we all wanted positive change for this school. We all could quite easily state *what* we wanted to change – that was the easy part. The difficult part was the *how* we are going to do it. We need to start short term and work long term. I started by saying, 'Unless someone can suggest a better way of tackling the problem this is how we are going to approach tomorrow.' – Breheney

Breheney describes herself as a passionate person who will not accept 'wrongs' lightly and will persist on a matter until she gets it right. Thus, despite fairly common advice that new principals should tread lightly initially, her first public statement of her 'vision' of safety, calm, good relationships and productivity within the school was made at the staff meeting held during the second week of the first term. What is more, this statement was accompanied by an announcement: 'Unless someone can suggest a better way of tackling the problem, this is how we are going to approach.'

The strategies that Breheney was suggesting were those adopted from two other schools in similar socioeconomic areas in Launceston with which she was familiar. At Mayfield, a small degree of success was noticeable almost immediately, and within a month quite a few of the staff were on side, in terms of accepting the likelihood of Breheney's vision being credible and in terms of the 'fit' of the sorts of strategies she had introduced in the second week of term.

Breheney championed the issue and the goal by articulating her vision at every staff meeting, through regular memoranda to staff, through newsletters to parents, through orations at school assemblies, and as part of her daily dialogue and distribution of rewards and sanctions. She implemented policies and programs, organised staff development and distributed resources in order to make Mayfield a better place for teaching and learning.

By the end of the first year about half the staff had come to share Breheney's vision. Of those teachers who stayed on for her second year, all had grabbed the vision as their own.

The development of a vision in the form of a document to be featured in the school plan is one thing; the visible evidence of its enactment is another and almost more crucially important

> Colleen's enthusiasm for change was contagious. We knew that she meant business when it came to making things better. It was obvious that teamwork and support was the key to achieving this success. – Staff member

matter. At the very least, the icons and rituals pervading the school and the language of the staff must be the vision made visible. Where actions do not match this rhetoric, there is great unease and incongruence.

STAFFING THE SCHOOL

By the end of the first year of her principalship, Breheney had significant influence over the composition of the school staff. In Tasmania's state education system, personnel matters are highly centralised. Nevertheless, Tasmania is a relatively small place and people at the centre, even if they have been in the state for just a short period of time, are well known – often on a personal level – and some individuals exercise influence on that centralised system through formal and informal means. Breheney was able to influence staffing at her school through her networks.

Some staff members, whether because they could not or would not become committed to the vision or for other reasons, successfully gained transfers to other schools at the end of the first year. Others teachers, at their own initiative, sought transfers into or initial appointments to the school. Some of these indicated that the main reason for their action was that they wanted to work with Breheney and her emerging team on what the grapevine indicated was a challenging, but ultimately possible task. Breheney was helped by sympathetic senior personnel such as district office superintendents to head-hunt other staff, some of whom had been her colleagues in the past.

EXTERNAL NETWORKS

The magnitude of the task at Mayfield was such that no school staff, no matter how single-minded they were or how collegially they went about their strategic and tactical activities, could hope for success without drawing on outsiders for help. Consequently, networks of various kinds were built and nurtured. District office personnel were central to these networks. During the early days of implementation, there were many, many demands for explanations from the Department of Education as a consequence of parents' complaints about the school. Breheney particularly remembers an incident when a parent complained directly to the minister for education about new procedures put in place for inappropriate behavior in the playground. As a consequence, the district superintendent telephoned Breheney to obtain the pertinent information, then talked to the dissatisfied parent at length before escorting her personally to visit other schools to observe similar practices in action. The superintendent also made herself available to talk with parent groups at the school in order to explain departmental policies and to demonstrate her support for Breheney and the staff generally.

> There were many ministerials in the early days. One of the first was over the consequences put in place for inappropriate behaviour in the playground. The parent strongly objected to the 'time-out seat' and stated that if her children were ever placed on this seat she would withdraw all her children from the school. – Breheney

Breheney also invited a range of politicians of all persuasions to visit the school in formal and informal capacities. Not only did this practice highlight the needs of the school, but it also indicated to the school's community that Mayfield Primary School was valued, and, significantly, it also suggested to parents that Breheney was supported in her actions. Furthermore, Breheney's unashamed display of contacts enabled her to persuade disgruntled parents to complain to her in the first instance rather than going immediately to the top: 'After all,' she'd explain, 'Tom or Mary will bring the matter to me, and sooner or later you and I will have to sit down and resolve the issue anyway; so we may as well start where we're going to finish.'

Breheney and her staff also liaised closely with principals and teachers of schools within the Launceston area with similar profiles to that of Mayfield, and regularly sought input from professional associations and consultants such as Bill Rogers and Maurice Balson. As an example, the strategies adopted to manage inappropriate student behavior early in Breheney's tenure were 'borrowed' in their entirety from her previous school. As these strategies were refined at Mayfield, the recent experiences of other schools were noted and consultants were employed to interact with staff because of their theory base and understanding of the broader picture.

> I really enjoyed the Northern Suburbs Cluster School's meetings with other staff. These bimonthly meetings gave us the opportunity to share strategies and ideas to help build positive procedures in our classrooms and playgrounds. – Pete, staff member

PROGRAM FIT

While Mayfield is similar in many ways to a large number of schools throughout Tasmania and elsewhere, it is also unique in others, including the strengths, fears and ambitions of staff and the particular balance of personalities among the students and the parents.

Thus, while some programs, especially in the early days, were adopted from other schools, the staff of Mayfield came to a strong belief that the programs, ultimately, had to fit Mayfield's unique situation.

There is no 'formula' for ensuring program fit, so Mayfield staff had to develop their own. One approach would have been to undertake research, analysis, debate and consensus-seeking prior to action, but this was not the method they adopted. The staff were convinced that doing something was the best approach.

By doing something, successes are achieved, and people learn much, have fun and develop a strong sense of *esprit de corps* from success.

Action, however, results in 'failure' from time to time. Again, though, astute people learn from their failures, can still have fun and can still develop strong bonds with their colleagues. Given this, Breheney and her staff refused to consider the likelihood of genuine failure – preferring to imagine that doing something would always lead to some sort of success in some sort of aspect of their professional and personal lives. At times staff would complain that 'It's just too hard.' Inevitably the response was: 'Certainly it's hard, but it's not as hard as not doing anything and suffering the consequences of such inaction.'

With positive thinking, psychological energy and persistence the programs outlined in the next chapter were nurtured and moulded until they worked at Mayfield for Mayfield's people.

It is instructive to consider the following comment made by a Year 5 boy to Mackrill soon after she joined Mayfield's staff:

> *'I may as well behave because Mrs Breheney and the others just don't let up! They keep at you and at you until you do it right.'*

Leadership through an organisational culture characterised by rights and responsibilities

Appropriate behavior by students based on individuals' rights and responsibilities, and non-violent management of it, was, and remains, a priority of the highest order in the school. This state of affairs is now generally regarded by school members as 'a reflection of their shared values, beliefs and commitments' (Sergiovanni 1991, p.218) and represents the staff's 'agreement, implicit or explicit, on how to approach decisions and problems: "The way things are done around here".' (Kilmann et al. 1985; 5). In short, Mayfield's emergent organisational culture describes and prescribes what school personnel do, especially when interpersonal behavior is the issue.

Mayfield Primary School staff have learnt ways of dealing with their work-a-day activities that have become more or less automatic. These ways are taught to newcomers formally, through professional development activities, and also more informally but no less powerfully through the rules, ceremonies, rituals, heroes and myths that have emerged over the past four or so years.

The school had had a basic code of ethics, which was described in a small document, for some time. However, this code did not drive the nature of the interpersonal relationships in the school and was judged by staff, parents and children of the day to be inadequate to meet the task of managing behavior.

Mayfield's playground behavior management policy was the first tactic in the battle to improve student–student and teacher–student relationships in the school. A clear sequence of steps to be taken in cases of inappropriate student behavior, ranging from conferencing and negotiating with students through to suspension for severe or violent behaviors was identified, discussed, agreed on, modelled for the teachers and practised by them.

There were problems during lunch and recess in the early days of the policy's implementation. Some children refused to go to the 'blue seat' for outside time-out or to the designated inside area for more serious breaches, and, at times, an excessive number of children were being directed to cram themselves onto or into these venues.

At an early staff meeting, teachers discussed and agreed on what behaviors were worthy of calling forth the time-out devices (see figure 1).

At the same time, teachers were instructed to remind children of appropriate playground behavior before *every* venture into the playground, and one-quarter of the staff were rostered on duty at any one time. The long-observed duty roster was changed from two teachers outside to two out and one in and, in addition, senior staff roved the playground and checked the time-out venues regularly.

While on duty, all teachers carried a notebook to write down the names of offenders and the nature of their offences, and these notes were used in subsequent interviews between students and their parents and senior staff and were useful in identifying children who were offending regularly in the playground.

These tactics, at the time, were regarded as mere 'quick fixes', and there was certainly no pretence that there was any attempt to

Figure 1:
Policy for behavior management in the playground
(adapted from Rogers 1995)

LEVEL 1	CONFERENCE STAFF/STUDENTS
• With the child or children. Stop and calm the child. • Questioning based on: 'What is the school rule?' • Listen to both sides of a problem. Each child gives his/her account with no interruptions. • Reflect back on the rule.	• Discuss what children are going to do about it. • Solutions are suggested by both parties. • Children choose the solution that is acceptable to them. • Children put solution into effect.

LEVEL 2	TIME-OUT OUTSIDE
• If further problems occur or child/children need to be removed from the area, direct them to time-out bench. • Children placed on time-out bench until duty teachers feel they can put the solution into operation.	• Name of the child/children is written in area duty book with comment about the problem. • Monitoring of children listed in book.

LEVEL 3	TIME-OUT INSIDE
• Children move to time-out area inside, located near the principal's office.	• Supervised by staff. Record problem in time-out book.

LEVEL 4	IMMEDIATE WITHDRAWL FROM PLAYGROUND
• Endangering others by throwing stones.	• Physical aggression making others unsafe.

LEVEL 5	PARENT INVOLVEMENT
• Major problem or continual disregard of school rules, parent/s will be contacted.	Discussion includes parents, senior staff and class teacher.

LEVEL 6	ADULT CONFERENCE
• Problem still occurring – need to discuss other methods that could be implemented	to modify behavior. Involve senior staff, class teacher, guidance officer, etc.

GENERAL COMMENTS	
• These procedures have been set in specific order, and understood and articulated by staff and children. The steps will bring about interaction between children and teachers in consistent behavior management. Methods determining incidents will be decided by the following guidelines:	**1 Minor incident** Work through each step of the behavior management process. Examples: spitting, pushing, not playing in the right areas. **2 Major incident** Related to safety aspect. Children to go straight to inside time-out. Examples: fighting, throwing stones.

teach children appropriate behaviors. However, teachers did welcome the policy because they viewed it as:

* systematic

* clear

* easy to implement

* offering potential for a short-term and (perhaps) a long-term solution to problems concerning relationships

Breheney also put in place a similar process by which classroom behaviors became a centre of attention (see figure 2).

Breheney convened a parent meeting to discuss the rights and responsibilities of parents in their dealings with the school. All parents were invited to the meeting through newsletters, and some parents whose children's behaviors were of greatest concern received personal invitations.

Just eight parents turned up to this meeting. However, this was not considered to be a disaster, as all parents are thought to be important in the educational process and here were eight potential allies in the cause. The meeting lasted for two hours and the group drew up a list of parental rights and responsibilities (see figure 3). The list was displayed prominently in the next newsletter and again throughout the year as the need arose, and the document was distributed to all new parents to the school. All parents were invited to classroom meetings in the first term, and the document was displayed and referred to by individual teachers on these occasions.

The various meetings involving parents were designed to entice more of them to participate in developing and enacting the school's policies, especially as they related to behavior management, and most parents had access to the document and were aware of its rationale and contents.

The document was not regarded simply as 'window dressing'; instead, it drove all the interactions with parents, especially those with dissenting or troublesome ones. It was a tool which was used frequently to remind parents of their rights and responsibilities and to focus discussion with them on relevant problems. Of course, there were times when individuals made claims such as 'I don't have to take notice of those things because I wasn't involved in their development.' The inevitable answer to this was something

Figure 2:
Behavior management in the classroom
(adapted from Rogers 1995)

	BEHAVIOR	TEACHER ACTION	EXTRA SUPPORT
LEVEL 1	Student respects the rights of self and others – is cooperative and self-controlled.	Reinforce behavior with appropriate comments and specific feedback (pat on the back, acknowledgment etc).	Involve colleagues in the celebration of children's achievements.
LEVEL 2	Basically respects the rights of others but has difficulties which affect own self-esteem. Some degree of frustration, low concentration levels creates **minor disruptions** (e.g. rudeness and annoying others, no homework, punctuality a problem, incorrect equipment.)	Teacher seeks solution to problem with student. Consultation with other colleagues, support staff and parents. Reinforce success, have behavior contracts between home and school, documentation given to support staff describing problem, class meetings.	If necessary, gain help from staff and principal in defining problem and applying solution.
LEVEL 3	Persistently violates the rights of others in a minor way. Has **continuing but minor problems**, e.g. violates rights of others, continues level 2 behavior, poor attitude to learning and work, rude and unresponsive in class.	Teacher consults with colleagues and support staff who may contact parents. Actions may include detention, consultation with appropriate support staff. Place on behavior contract, withdraw from playground or school functions.	Involve support from colleagues, support staff, principal, welfare officer, etc.
LEVEL 4	**Continually breaches the rights of others.** Regular and serious infringements of the rights of others, e.g. verbal or physical assault, intimidation, vandalism, defiance, disruption, etc. Isolated serious breaking of rules, continues deterioration in behavior, ignoring any attempts to help.	Teacher consults with colleagues and support staff who contact parents. Documentation recorded and filed. Information passed to all staff. Actions include child being banned from school functions, internal suspension (followed by counselling and contract), no playground privileges, time-out, daily behavior report.	Must involve support staff, principal, guidance officer and parent. Case conference a suggested option.
LEVEL 5	**Seriously violates the rights of others and shows no signs of wanting to change**, e.g. abusive, poor effect on peers, dangerous, uncontrollable and uncooperative.	Teacher refers problem directly to principal. After discussion with parents, student may be suspended.	Must involve principal, parent, guidance officer, and district education officer.

like 'Well, here's a copy of the newsletters (or personal communication) that went home to you and you chose not to be involved. If you're content to allow other parents to determine these things for you, that's okay; but if you want your views heard then please contribute in a positive manner through the Parents and Friends Association, class meetings and other forums.'

The rights and responsibilities of students were also documented. To this end, all teachers were instructed to prepare, in consultation with their students, a written statement of rights and responsibilities relevant to the classroom and the school more generally. These individual contributions were discussed at a staff meeting and this discussion led to the distillation and refinement

RIGHTS OF PARENTS	RESPONSIBILITIES OF PARENTS
I have the right to ...	*I have the responsibility to ...*
• have the school communicate information about my children and the school in general	• regularly keep in contact with the teachers and the school in general
• be kept informed of my children's progress	• support the education of my children, to make every effort to be kept informed and respond if there is a need
• be treated with respect and have my opinions valued	• be involved in the activities of the school
• be part of the decision-making of the school	• ensure the time taken to be informed does not take teachers away from teaching duties and class responsibilities
• assist with formulating of school policies and rules	• respect the staff of the school and value their professional opinions
• receive positive feedback about the education of my child and the school in general	• support the school in decisions made, and to process and promote them actively to my children and the community
• have my children learn to their potential	• talk positively about my children's school to my children and the community in general
• expect that my children work in a clean, orderly and tidy environment	• act as a partner with the school to help my children learn to their potential
• know that my children are going to a school where pride in the school, including work and the way they are dressed, is promoted	• make every effort to understand the programs being offered to my children
	• help keep the environment clean
	• ensure my children are well dressed and prepared for school

Figure 3:
Rights and responsibilities of parents

of a list. This list was taken back to every classroom (K–6) for discussion, clarification and ultimate ratification by the students. (See figure 4.)

These rights and responsibilities became a real focus point in all aspects of the school's operations which were directly relevant to students. The list was featured prominently in classrooms, in hallways, in senior staff offices and elsewhere. Children's work was displayed and created around items on the list and such work often involved consideration of some aspect of them.

The children were reminded of the contents of the list and the

RIGHTS OF CHILDREN	RESPONSIBILITIES OF CHILDREN
I have the right to ...	*I have the responsibility to ...*
• feel safe and happy	• make others feel safe and happy
• learn	• help others learn
• be treated as a person with respect	• respect other people
• know that my property is safe	• respect and care for other people's property
• work in a clean and tidy school	• make sure I help to keep our school clean and tidy

reason for them regularly throughout the day and, of course, it was used as a starting point for discussion of any inappropriate behavior.

It made us look more deeply at our role in this process. – Liz, staff member

If children have rights, and parents have rights it follows that teachers should have rights too. This was empowering for us as a staff. – Kathy, staff member

Students' rights and responsibilities **saturated** daily events in that all attitudinal, behavioral and academic considerations regarding students were driven by them.

Teachers at the school also recognised that they, as well as parents and students, have rights and responsibilities, and at about the same time as the foregoing activities were taking place Breheney invited a staff member to chair a staff meeting at which a number of teachers' rights and responsibilities were identified. This list (see figure 5) was, in turn, discussed at

MAKING PEACE AT MAYFIELD

RIGHTS OF STAFF	RESPONSIBILITIES OF STAFF	
I have the right to ...	*I have the responsibility to ...*	Figure 5: Rights and responsibilities of staff

RIGHTS OF STAFF

I have the right to ...

- feel valued as a person and as a professional
- teach without disruption
- be shown courtesy and consideration by all in the school community
- work in a safe, supportive environment
- have the support of parents of the children I teach
- have the opportunity to carry out and evaluate a program that caters for all the children in my class
- have the opportunity for my own professional development
- have my property respected
- work in a clean, tidy and orderly environment

RESPONSIBILITIES OF STAFF

I have the responsibility to ...

- make every effort to value others in the school community
- ensure a professional approach to my work
- provide a quality education program
- treat all in the school whether parents, teachers or children with care, courtesy and consideration
- offer support to senior staff and colleagues
- promote a safe, supportive environment for others
- continually inform parents of the program I conduct with their children and the progress they are making, and offer them opportunities to be involved
- allocate appropriate time to plan
- ensure success for all children
- actively involve myself in resource allocation and program budgeting of the school
- take responsibility for my professional development
- respect the property of others
- promote a clean, tidy and orderly environment and take responsibility for common areas e.g. art areas,

Figure 5:
Rights and
responsibilities of staff

meetings with parents and in class with children, and displayed prominently in the staff room and at several other highly visible places in the school.

As with the parents' and students' rights and responsibilities, the teachers' list was used as a tool – in teachers' personal reflections, in their interactions with senior staff concerning their professional development, and in their interplay with parents and students.

Improvement through a focus on professional and curriculum development

Although we have mainly concentrated so far on a range of beliefs and policies, we are not suggesting that Mayfield's changed condition was due entirely to such matters. On the contrary, it is our belief that change in people on the staff, through professional development activities and consequent reflection and experimentation, was responsible in no small way for the improvement in the school environment. Policies on individuals' rights and responsibilities, alone, are mere bandaids. They may give an impression that ills have been overcome, but ultimately bandaids fall off or otherwise cease to hide root causes of those ills. School improvement requires changes in the assumptions and behaviors of the staff, and such changes do not come easily.

Following Miles (1987), we argue that good ideas will see the light of day in classrooms when five conditions are satisfied. The first of these is that would-be implementers must be abundantly **clear** about the meaning and nature of what is to be implemented. The second is that they must see the matter as being **relevant** to them in their situation. The third and fourth are that they must possess the **skill** and the **will** to bring the change into their active repertoires. We cannot see anything novel or startling in these four conditions, but a fifth one, we believe, is thought of rarely. It is that people need to be assisted to develop **positive mental images** of themselves 'doing' the new activity.

Mental image, despite being a loosely defined, vague and fuzzy construct (Grady 1993), is an important factor in people's thinking and behavior. A person's mental images represent what might be called his or her subjective knowledge of 'fact' and 'value' (Boulding 1956). These images are theories in use (Argyris & Schon 1978), and are largely metaphorical in nature (Morgan 1986). Significantly, these images seem to shape what is seen (Morgan 1983), are acquired, in part at least, through the 'universe of discourse' and are influenced by the belief that the images are shared by other people like oneself (colleagues, for example).

At Mayfield, therefore, Breheney and her senior staff judged that good quality professional development was unlikely to eventuate when staff read, experimented, practised, reflected and so on largely in isolation. The school's leaders nurtured collegial interaction and inquiry, and, ultimately, commitment to such activity emerged. A critical factor was the separate involvement of parents and teachers during the first year in a series of workshops led by well-known author and consultant Maurice Balson. The major focus of these occasions was a consideration of Balson's (1987) assumptions regarding behavior management:

1 All behavior has social meaning – no behavior should be isolated from its social context.

2 Belonging is the basic need – all behavior by students represents their efforts to gain status or recognition.

3 All behavior is purposeful – we make decisions, consciously or, more often, unconsciously and we must look to purposes of behavior and not to the causal reasons for it.

4 Feelings of inferiority lie behind all disturbing behavior.

This is not to say that these sorts of assumptions were necessarily new to Mayfield staff or to teachers generally. During the mid 1980s in Tasmania, and elsewhere around the world, there was a growing concern at the incidence of children who were exhibiting seriously worrying behaviors in primary schools.

Studies made in response to this concern indicated that characteristics such as poor concentration; aggression; wandering and inability to stay on task; noisy, disruptive and disobedient attention-seeking; and destructiveness were all typical of children who were causing teachers and senior staff a great deal of concern (e.g. Tasmanian Early Childhood Senior Staff Association 1986). Strategies for use in the classrooms of behaviorally difficult children were also developed (e.g. Collis & Dalton 1990).

In the early 1990s, the Tasmanian Department of Education and the Arts seconded a number of teachers from their schools to assist with the implementation of a supportive school environment program. Mayfield Primary School used to the full the expertise and experience of these seconded teachers, and invited them to work alongside teachers in the classrooms and to help with the running of professional development sessions in the school.

Other professional development workshops were given prominence in the staff's activities as well. Sometimes these were led by members of staff who had something to offer, perhaps as a result of attending a conference or participating in some sort of activity away from the school. At other times, consultants were contracted to support the staff, to appraise approaches being tried, and to help modify and polish products and processes associated with managing conflict and anger, and the teaching of cooperation skills.

Common understandings of possible explanations for behavior – such as frustration and children's inability to deal with it in a socially acceptable manner – and ways of managing this emerged and, importantly, these workshops highlighted the fact that schools like Mayfield were not alone in the problems and difficulties they were experiencing.

Bill Rogers has had a significant impact on the staff's beliefs and modus operandi. Teachers had face-to-face access in the school to Rogers and his work for four successive years. His approach fits well with the teachers, parents and staff of Mayfield, and, what's more, these people were willing and able to adopt the general thrust of the approach. Not only did Rogers lead in workshop settings but he also worked in the classroom with teachers, modelling strategies and suggesting solutions.

A feature of the school calendar each year is the allocation of two full days before the children return after the Christmas holidays for staff to engage in professional development activities relevant to behavior management. Staff with particular expertise in aspects such as the conduct of classroom meetings lead their returning colleagues, as they revisit their behavior management strategies, and their newly appointed colleagues as they acquire expertise in 'the Mayfield way'.

Throughout the year, the principal and other staff members sometimes put other matters aside to model appropriate strategies in classrooms, while interschool visits by staff and parents, mentoring systems, and a craftsman/apprentice model ensure that there is an ongoing focus on behavior matters.

In 1992, the staff implemented a formal system of teacher appraisal for professional development purposes. The system involved self-selected 'buddies' engaging in cycles of pre-observation conference to agree on aspects to be observed, observation and collection of data relevant to the agreed focus of the observation, and post-observation conference and training where deemed necessary. Within twelve months, though, this practice was discontinued as staff members, through the gradual formation of personal networks and support systems within the school, developed other more informal processes.

While managing and teaching appropriate behaviors, *per se*, was given highest priority, staff meetings and other professional development activities were also devoted to a range of curriculum issues relevant to the broad picture and to particular aspects which were of concern to teachers at the time. Teaching and content were examined to ensure their congruence with children's academic and behavioral needs, and the curriculum came to include material concerned with children's behavior. In the language program, for example, children talked and wrote about relationships, consequences and appropriate behavior. The curriculum was doing double duty, and a broad range of student concerns were catered for simultaneously. Staff also engaged in professional development activities that featured methods of teaching and ways of grouping children as well as consideration for learning styles and preferences.

Modelling of exemplary teaching practice and organisation was another important component of the professional development program at Mayfield. This process served two purposes. Firstly, individual teachers were acknowledged by peers, senior staff, district office personnel, parents and politicians, and their work was celebrated at morning teas, through written feedback from senior staff and others, and through being invited to demonstrate a skill, for example, to groups of teachers in the school or in other schools. Secondly, strategies were learned which helped ensure continuity and consistency of philosophy and practice. Thus, if a child refused to work on an activity, for example, the usual practice was to offer him or her a number of choices such as 'You can do it now, or at lunchtime, or when the rest of the class goes to ...', but the final outcome was not negotiable; that is, 'It has to be done'.

This focus on the teaching and learning environment was essential to ensure that appropriate consideration was given to all elements of the educational program. An important premise is that the curriculum must fit the children, rather than the children fit the curriculum. The following features were considered to be essential for a successful program for children at Mayfield, and in particular for behaviorally difficult children.

- The content of the program must have relevance to the children, in that they should be able to see that it will be important and useful to them in the future.

- Teachers must be flexible in their teaching approach and monitor the mood or atmosphere in the class continually. For example, if the children are uninterested or restless, teachers should consider implementing some more or less active experience to either provide a break or to re-stimulate interest and concentration.

- The program must cater for individual learning styles and needs. Some children need a more structured and prescribed program, others work effectively on self-initiated experiences. Some children may be able to concentrate on skills-based experiences like spelling or number work immediately, whereas for others it may be more appropriate to engage in some sort of self-expression like painting, drawing or work with clay before they tackle the more formal tasks. A skilled teacher will be perceptive to these individual needs and ensure that the program is varied, child-centred and individually focused.

- The successful classrooms, shared areas and corridors at Mayfield feature a clear, uncluttered and aesthetically pleasing sense of order. This serves two purposes. Firstly, it enables the display of children's work to be of the highest quality, precisely mounted and prepared for sharing with others, and a sign of the real valuing of children's work. It serves as a clear indication that the children's successes are being celebrated. Similarly, clarity is the feature of the display of classroom rules, merit charts and the like. This clarity and order makes for a very relaxed and almost peaceful atmosphere. The second purpose for such order and emphasis away from a cluttered or over-stimulated environment is that it is very much a 'self-serving' environment, where children can easily gain access to all the materials and resources they need without being distracted, wasting time, or interrupting others to get what they require

Improvement through parent education and participation

Involvement of parents as partners in the educative process was a key ingredient of Breheney's personal vision and of the emergent shared vision for the school. The partnership was to be founded on:

- education of parents concerning their rights and responsibilities

- raising of parents' awareness of the school's programs
- building positive relationships and mutual supportiveness between parents and staff
- resolution of conflict between parents where their relationships impinged on the school's effectiveness
- counselling of parents on a wide variety of matters

Early in Breheney's tenure, all but a few visits by parents to the school were for the purpose of making complaints about a variety of matters. Some of these were to do with treatment of children and other aspects related to schooling, but others were concerned primarily with relationships beyond the school's jurisdiction, such disputes between neighbors. Of course Breheney always dealt with these complaints, but she insisted that parents must also visit the school for positive reasons to view and celebrate their children's achievements and to witness the many other positive things happening in the school. Indeed, Breheney would regularly utter invitations such as 'Well, you're here now, so let's go and have a look at some good things in your child's classroom.'

Also all teachers agreed to communicate regularly to parents all the positive occurrences at the school. This was accomplished in a variety of ways, for example:

- 'Thought you'd like to know' notes
- photocopying and sending home good work
- home visits
- phone calls
- merit certificates awarded to children
- profiling of students' work and sending these profiles home at the end of each term
- open days/nights
- distribution of the school newsletter *Mayday*
- encouraging parent help in classrooms
- individual class meetings
- parent workshops and seminars

Social occasions with parents were also a regular feature in the school's calendar. These were often in the form of family barbecues, sporting activities such as a staff versus parents softball match and an annual bush dance to which parents and other members of the school's community were invited.

Staff identified a number of parents whose behavior and negative attitudes towards the school were of serious concern. It was agreed to use proactive measures with this group. Staff members made particular efforts to seek out and talk with these people and to convey positive messages as frequently as possible. If their children experienced any problems at school, the parents would always be contacted by telephone or through a home visit to convey the school's version of the problem before the child got home.

The foundation for effective parent participation, though, needs to be built on good, trusting relationships, at the heart of which is people's need to feel valued. Two of the tactics adopted by Breheney to foster such a foundation were highly symbolic. One was that she invited every adult to use her first name, and, as a consequence, was addressed as 'Colleen', even when the name was accompanied by a string of invectives alluding to her parentage, habits and other attributes. The second was that she relocated her office.

Breheney had inherited an office at the rear of the reception area, which, itself, was guarded by a sliding glass partition and a closed door. The principal's is now the very first door that is seen when anyone comes into the vestibule, and that door is always open unless private counselling or other such activities are in process.

At the beginning of every school year, all parents are invited into the school for group or individual meetings with class teachers, and those parents who do not attend such meetings are contacted by telephone or personal note. Thus, within the first three or four weeks, significant contact regarding school policies and processes is made with at least one parent of every child in the school.

Regular contacts with parents are nurtured throughout the year as well through, for example, all teachers sending 'I thought you'd like to know' notes home with children or through other means, and via a regular newsletter. A specific example is that at one time the students decided that they would raise money to buy some playground equipment and decided to mount an exhibition of their art work. Personnel from district office, politicians, and other public figures were invited. Many parents came to this function and were thereby witness to considerable initiative, goodwill and profit-making.

Another program responsible for forming strong bonds with families is the Early School program. District office provided Mayfield, and other selected schools, with some additional staffing amounting to one teacher day per week to implement a program for children who were identified as being 'at risk' developmentally and who were younger than the specified school starting age. These children were selected through advice from the child health clinic or from knowledge of the family via siblings who were already in the school.

The Early School program has two components. The first is a school-based session of no longer than two hours which is run by the teacher with some parent help as support. No more than eight children attend this session at one time. The carefully planned program provides valuable cognitive, social and physical experiences for the children while modelling appropriate strategies and behaviors for the parents. While parents watch, the teacher may engage the children in imaginative play, games which focus on gross motor skills, and group work which involves taking turns and sharing resources.

The second component is a home-based program in which the teacher visits each of the children who attend the school-based session, and other children who for some reason cannot attend or are not confident to attend the school-based session. The teacher visits each child in the home and takes with them a selection of materials and equipment in order to model to the parent the forms of interaction between adults and children that are demonstrated within the school. There is no doubt the positive relationships formed between the teacher, parent and child are invaluable to future school-based involvement.

Parents participate in Mayfield Primary School business at various levels. These levels include visiting the school to complain, or to celebrate success; working on craft stalls or helping in the canteen; working with children in classrooms; and being involved in decision- and policy-making.

Tasmanian state schools are not obliged to form school councils, and Mayfield has not constituted one to date. Parents, consequently, have limited legitimate power and authority in the formal education of their children. Nevertheless, there is much encouragement for parents to become involved, and advice to the principal through, for example, the parents and friends group is normally acted upon. Many parents have developed various capacities, such as engaging in debate and decision-making, through their involvement in the school.

> Some schools had followed this pathway [school councils]. Mayfield did not regard it as a priority as compared to other issues, and were more than happy with the processes for decision-making and parent involvement as they were. – Parent

As with other important aspects such as behavior man-agement, curriculum refinement and staff development, the parental side of the partnership continues to be nurtured. At the time of writing, for example, the school staff, with assistance from a contracted consultant, is conducting a major investigation of parent capacities, concerns and needs as a precursor to a major re-examination of the language program, within which it is thought that parents will be required to play a more significant role than has been customary to date.

Whole school and classroom programs

3

THE PROGRAMS DESCRIBED in this chapter, and their associated ideas and strategies, have been developed over a period of time, and are being continually appraised and refined to ensure that they are still relevant and beneficial to the students at Mayfield.

It is important for any teacher or school administrator to understand that the programs outlined here are not to be considered as 'quick fixes' or 'recipes' for the management of violent behaviors in schools. They must be viewed merely as components of an overall school strategy – important components that, coupled with a commitment to a supportive school ethos, blend together with aspects of management, leadership and collaborative engagement to enhance school effectiveness. They are not 'band-aids' to patch 'injuries' and 'sore spots', but are well thought-out, tested procedures that have been developed, redeveloped, polished, experimented with, supported and implemented by committed staff.

This view would be supported by Miles (1987), who claims that 'Successful change is most likely when the program is evolutionary rather than tightly pre-designed.' It is important that programs, ideas and strategies are not accepted simply because they have proved to be successful in another setting. Program 'fit' needs to be established through trial and adaptation; by doing rather than by planning.

Given the behaviors which exemplified Mayfield's dark side, the staff, through close observation and action research, believed that children's negative behaviors resulted primarily from the following four problem areas:

- **poor interpersonal skills** and the consequent inability to establish and maintain friendships with others, and the inability of many children to communicate in a positive, non-aggressive manner with peers and adults

- **low self-esteem**, in that many children failed to see themselves as people of worth

- **inability to channel negative feelings** in a socially acceptable manner

- **inability to handle conflict** in a non-aggressive way and a failure to understand the consequences of their actions

The Supportive School Environment program

With these four problem areas in mind, the staff worked together to design a whole-school program, called the Supportive School Environment program, to be led by a specialist teacher.

A supportive school environment program is more than simply the management of behavior. It is about the development of a supporting and caring school; a school that is deeply concerned about all its members; a school that encourages shared decision-making, and genuine collaboration; and a school that works hard at making all people feel of worth and of value. In a truly supportive environment, you will see people demonstrating care and concern for each other through good relationships, by the words that are spoken, and by the actions that are undertaken. A supportive school environment features quality relationships between all members of the community. The supportive element – support between children, staff and parents – is the key to success.

The aims of this program at Mayfield are to:

- heighten the profile of the supportive school environment ethos in the school

- teach positive and effective social skills to children

- teach appropriate problem-solving skills to children

- provide experiences to facilitate the development of a positive self-image in children

- teach strategies for relationship building

- teach anger management techniques and conflict resolution skills

ORGANISATION OF THE SUPPORTIVE SCHOOL ENVIRONMENT PROGRAM

The staff believed that if this program was to be successful, it must have top priority for funding. They made a unanimous decision to use two days a week of their staffing allocation to employ a resource teacher for extra time to work with all classes from Kindergarten to Year 6.

The role of this resource teacher is to:

- conduct scheduled sessions with all classes from K to 6

- act as a resource for classroom teachers

- conduct professional development sessions for staff to help them develop relevant skills and knowledge

- provide support to families by running parent sessions and visiting homes

- work intensively with individual children or small groups who display severe behavior problems

Each class spends one hour per fortnight working in a room specifically organised for the purposes of the program. This fortnightly session for each class is co-planned by the classroom teacher and the resource teacher. The work undertaken during these sessions is then revisited continually and practised persistently in the classroom and in the playground.

The program works because it receives total commitment from all staff members and elicits high quality cooperation among them.

Although the resource teacher is funded in part for this purpose, she is a full-time member of staff who has other responsibilities to make up the remainder of her load. This arrangement ensures consistency and continuity for teachers and children, in that the resource teacher is able to model and discuss relevant skills with them throughout the entire week.

TOWARDS A COMMON GOAL: ACTIVITIES AND STRATEGIES IN THE SCHEDULED SESSIONS

Activities within the scheduled fortnightly sessions of the program focus on children working together towards a common goal. Cooperative learning enables teachers to shift from a simple didactic style of teaching to one where emphasis is placed on interaction and interdependence in a positive classroom atmosphere.

1 Whole-class games

The objective here is to facilitate the acquisition of cooperative skills such as taking turns, working as a team, acknowledging the strengths of others, and positive communication, as well as understanding the importance of supporting and encouraging others in the cooperative process.

Many of these games focus on self-esteem, and involve giving and receiving compliments, or interacting with each other in non-threatening ways, such as holding hands in Pass the Squeeze. In this game the children sit in a circle holding hands. The objective of the game is to receive and pass a hand squeeze around the circle as quickly as possible. The teacher starts by squeezing a hand of a child next to her and at the same time starting a stop-watch. The class works together to see if they can reduce the time it takes to pass the squeeze around the circle.

2 Problem-solving and values clarification

Problem-solving on behavioral issues in the Supportive School Environment room. A group session: 'What would I do if ...'

Through the process of brainstorming, children discuss real-life problems, issues or challenges. Starting points could be quality literature, a picture stimulus, or the selection of a problem stated on a card. Every student's contribution is encouraged and valued and each suggestion is discussed by the students, who examine consequences and accept or reject or refine the ideas.

3 Paired or small group work

Paired and small group work encourages each participant to take shared

responsibility in decision-making. A variety of strategies can be used to select children to work in pairs or small groups, such as people who are born on the same date or in the same month, people with the same number of letters in their name, or people with the same favorite color.

4 Individual work and learning centres

Individual work gives children practice in reflecting on their own ideas and thoughts. The products of this work can then be shared with the rest of the class and added to the child's bank of work, or used in a profile or record of development.

Learning centres or work stations are set up around the special purpose room with an individual focus or

Paired work in the Supportive School Environment program. 'I will / I won't'

challenge, and are also an important part of the program. They focus on activities such as 'Look at the picture of this person. How do you think they are feeling? Draw or write about what you think could have happened to make them feel that way'; 'Write a compliment note to a friend. Post it in the post box'; or 'Choose one of the books from the basket. Which one do you think has the happiest story? Write down why you think it is the happiest.'

FOCUSING ON AREAS OF CONCERN: PRACTICAL SUGGESTIONS FOR THE CLASSROOM

Strategies associated with the whole-school program are also used in normal classrooms and involve activities that require, for example, thoughtful discussion, written work, art work, games and role play. Some practical suggestions for the classroom based on the four identified areas of concern outlined above are offered below.

RELATIONSHIP-BUILDING ACTIVITIES

1 Students develop and answer a questionnaire entitled 'How well do I know my friend?' Questions are included about birth date and favorite colors, foods, hobbies, television programs etc. The completed questionnaire is then shown to the friend and the responses are evaluated by the pair of students.

2 Students make their own autograph books and then ask others for their autographs, with the requirement that something nice is written, e.g. 'To Bill who is a great friend – Angela'.

3 Students write letters to others in the class and tell them something positive about them and why they are liked .

4 Books such as Judy Blume's *The Pain and The Great One*, Bob Graham's *Rose Meets Mr Wintergarden* and Michael Foreman's *Cat and Mouse Love Story* and *Cat and Canary* can be used to stimulate discussion, writing or drawing about relationships.

SELF-ESTEEM ACTIVITIES

1 Make class big books with topics such as:

We are special because ....

My favorite warm fuzzy is ....

I am good at....

2 Students make their own Super Star Chart which has a photograph or drawing of themselves in the middle of a large sheet of paper. Classmates are then invited to write some positive comments about the 'star' around the photograph or drawing.

A learning centre focused on relationship building. 'How to make friends'

3 Students make 'me' books or posters. Comments on things like my family, my shoe size, my favorite food, my favorite book, my favorite video, my favorite television program, my fingerprints, my height, my weight, my favorite toy are included. Groups or the whole class share and discuss the books.

4 Students make up a Who am I? about somebody else in the class. Five positive things are written about the person such as:

I am good at football

I am a fast runner

I have long tidy hair

I am kind to others

I try hard to improve my writing

Who am I?

Authors read them out to the class and students, in turn, try to identify the person.

5 Students discuss their names and ask questions such as 'Do you like your name ?', 'Why do you feel this way?', 'What do you think is the origin and meaning of your name?'

6 Students play a whole-class compliment game. The class sits in a circle and each child takes it in turn to role a ball to another class member. The sender needs to say something nice about the receiver, e.g. 'I like the way you try hard to spell correctly.' The recipient needs to reply 'Thank you.' Eye contact between giver and receiver is important throughout such activities.

7 Quality children's books such as *Willy the Wimp* and *Mouse with the Too Long Tail* can be used to good effect to stimulate discussion about the nature, causes and consequences of positive self-esteem.

FEELINGS

1 The teacher writes a number of problems or events on individual cards and places them in a basket. For example, 'Someone calls you a nasty name in the playground', or 'Your pet has died', or 'You have just come first in a race'. A child is chosen to select a card and role-play the emotion he or she might feel. A class member describes the way the child is feeling.

2 Use 'feelings dice' or 'feelings cards'. Students sit in a circle and take turns to flip over a card or throw dice, and then describe a time when they felt the emotion shown on the card or dice. The student then describes how they dealt with that feeling at the time, says whether or not those actions helped, and indicates what alternative or supplementary actions could have been taken.

3 Students make big books or posters in small or whole-class groups which describe all the ways they could deal appropriately with negative emotions. These books or posters are displayed clearly and referred to often.

4 Students make a poster by cutting photographs of people's faces out of magazines. They then explain how they think these people are feeling, predict why they are feeling this way, and classify the various emotions into groups.

5 Children's books, such as *John Brown, Rose and the Midnight Cat, I'll Always Love You* and *Nobody Asked Me If I Wanted a Baby Sister*, as in the other focus areas, offer excellent stimuli for discussing feelings.

A learning centre focused on feelings. 'I am sad when ...'

CONFLICT RESOLUTION

1 Children are encouraged to discuss real conflict situations that have occurred in the classroom or in the playground and are helped to identify and decide on appropriate strategies for resolving such conflicts in a constructive manner. Appropriate behaviors are role-played and practised again and again. This practice is often embodied in the daily contract for all students

in a particular class where students write about their behavior and read and discuss their product with others.

2 The teacher engages students in the STOP THINK DO technique (Petersen & Gannoni 1992), by which, for example, when addressing the problem 'What will you do when a person pushes in front of you in a line?' students are encouraged to:

stop: assess the situation

think: decide on three possible actions, thinking carefully about the potential consequences of each of these actions

do: implement the most appropriate action

The traffic light symbol is used to remind students of the process, and is displayed prominently around the school.

3 Signposting to behavior
The teacher presents the children with a problem situation such as 'What will you do when someone threatens to "get you" after school today?' The children write down and discuss with a friend three positive things that could be done in this situation and three things that it would be inappropriate to do. They then evaluate the alternatives, and select and justify the best one.

4 Discussion
Students discuss the nature and merit of rules that exist at school, at home, in the street and elsewhere; identify similarities and differences in rules in various situations; enumerate consequences of breaking these rules. Children also identify sources of rules and legitimate ways and means of changing rules.

5 Role-play
Students can role-play a parliamentary, council, club or family meeting and formulate a new rule (law), and then defend it against probes from the teacher or someone else.

The Lunchtime program

The Lunchtime program was devised by the specialist physical education teacher, in consultation with senior staff, to reduce the severe levels of aggressive behavior exhibited by students in the schoolground, particularly at lunchtimes. The general approach is to offer a greater range of sports and other outdoor activities for the children at these times. The staff judged that in order for these sports and activities to be successful and to inhibit any conflict or disagreement among children, close supervision would be necessary. This supervision is provided in the following ways:

- peer support leaders, selected annually and trained in handling behavioral problems, are rostered to run the activities

- two teachers at a time, who are all well aware of the peer support leaders' role and who are all prepared and skilled to follow up behavioral problems when requested by a leader, are rostered on duty

- a teachers' aide takes small groups of children for various activities

- the specialist physical education teacher monitors the organisational aspects of the program and also acts as another duty teacher

- senior staff move about the school and the grounds whenever possible

THE ROLE OF THE PHYSICAL EDUCATION TEACHER

One person needs to be responsible for this program. At Mayfield it is organised by the PE teacher, whose responsibilities are to:

- choose the peer support leaders

- teach peer support leaders and other children physical, social and organisational skills

- roster the leaders and display this roster each week

- organise equipment

- follow up problems the leaders experience

- remind leaders of the nature and location of their duty each lunchtime over the school's public address system

- oversee the program each and every lunchtime

PEER SUPPORT LEADERS

There are as many peer support programs as there are schools, and this name is given to any number of programs, some of which have a very specific rationale and established guidelines. The program at Mayfield is fairly simplistic in nature, but very effective in function.

Each lunchtime about eight peer support leaders are on roster. It is their responsibility to:

- collect the equipment they need from a central storage area at the beginning of lunchtime

- be at a designated area for the activity for which they have responsibility for the entire lunchtime

- supervise and/or umpire the activity to which they have been scheduled

- collect and return the equipment at the end of lunchtime

An observer of a good peer support leader in action could be forgiven for thinking that they were watching a person with far more leadership skills than an average 10- or 11-year-old. One peer support leader could be delivering an umpiring decision decisively, another could be explaining the rules of behavior for an errant child, while yet another could be modifying an activity to suit the ages of the children in their group. The range of skills and abilities they need to either possess or develop is extensive. The leaders themselves see the peer support program as a rewarding experience.

A peer support umpire at work

'It's fun, especially when a lot of kids come and you can get a good game going.' (Kane)

'We enjoy helping in the yard, and there are a lot less fights now.' (Conrad)

SELECTION AND TRAINING OF PEER SUPPORT LEADERS

The physical education teacher chooses approximately 40 potential peer support leaders from Years 3 to 6 at the start of each year, and then rosters each of them for one or two sessions per week.

The children who are chosen to be leaders work, in a master–apprentice fashion, alongside the PE teacher during some normal physical education lessons. This enables the leaders to learn the skills and the procedures for the activities, and allows all children to know who the peer support leaders are. In some lessons, the leaders not only acquire the skill components of various sports and activities (e.g. dribbling, passing and goal-shooting for basketball), but also develop competence in coaching others in those skills.

Often two or three classes are combined to make sure that groups are large enough to create a lunchtime 'feel', and peer support leaders practise supervision, umpiring and coaching skills in exactly the same way as they would during the lunchtime. The only significant difference between these practice sessions and the real lunchtime settings is that in the practice sessions groups of children rotate around the various activities on a signal from the physical education teacher. In the relative calm of a physical education lesson, potential conflict situations can be monitored closely by the teacher, who may choose to let children and peer support leaders sort out problems by themselves, or may intervene to model mediation behavior and counsel a troublesome participant, in much the same way as would happen at lunchtime if a leader needed help from one of the adults who would be nearby.

For the junior primary (K–2) physical education classes, some peer support leaders need to be withdrawn from their regular classroom programs to take groups, under the supervision of the PE teacher. Although this means that these peer support leaders miss out on their normal academic curriculum time for up to three or four hours per school term, this practice is deemed necessary for two reasons:

- the younger children need to build up a rapport with the leaders before they feel confident to approach them at lunchtimes

- the younger children need to engage in the various activities in their actual location with a leader in order for them to clearly realise that the activity is for them at lunchtime

MOTIVATING PEER SUPPORT LEADERS

While most of the peer support leaders are motivated intrinsically by the thrill of being in a leadership role, they are given a high profile in the school, and the teachers and the other students regard it as an honor to be chosen.

Their efforts are acknowledged in many ways: through announcements at assemblies, through the award of certificates at the end of the year, through acknowledgment in the school newsletter, and through being invited to a special peer support picnic. Their role and responsibilities in the playground are well understood by the whole school community, and they are easily recognised because of the specially named caps they wear.

EXAMPLES OF ACTIVITIES

1 Games for junior primary

One leader organises a simple running type game (i.e. stuck-in-mud); leader ensures that children play fairly.

2 Skipping for junior primary

Two leaders turn a long rope for junior primary children and give out small ropes to be used in a designated area; leaders ensure safe use of ropes.

4 Football for junior primary

One leader supervises the use of about 10 plastic footballs; children kick end to end; leader ensures there is no pushing or tackling.

5 Bats and balls – all students

One leader distributes bats and balls to children who wish to use them in a variety of ways, e.g. for Totem Tennis, Mini Tennis, Hit-up Wall (similar to handball except against a wall like squash without a racquet); leader ensures equipment is used in designated area and returned.

6 Basketball – years 3–4

One leader umpires a loosely structured game; leader ensures a fair, safe game.

7 Football – years 5–6

One leader umpires a game; leader ensures a fair, safe game.

8 Newcome ball (modified volleyball) – years 3–4

One leader umpires and scores game; leader ensures a fair, safe game.

The basis of each activity's format is planned carefully by the PE teacher and negotiated with the children, and from time to time renegotiation is required.

Peer support leaders teaching early childhood children a skipping game

A TYPICAL LUNCHTIME

The bell for lunch goes at 12.30 pm, at which time classroom teachers each supervise their own children while they eat in the classroom. A second bell at 12.40 signals that children are allowed to go into the grounds. Immediately, many opportunities for constructive play will be obvious to them. Aside from the fixed play equipment, the peer support leaders will be in position ready to take activities. Students can choose whether or not to take part in these activities.

Six or seven activities run concurrently, and are located at various points around the grounds. One or two leaders umpire or supervise each activity. Some activities are specific to particular age groups, while others are not. All are gender inclusive.

There is extensive supervision of the grounds. The two teachers on duty perform much the same function as at other schools. However, a strong, positive working relationship between the duty teachers and the six or seven peer support leaders is imperative. If a peer support leader approaches a duty teacher with a problem (for example, if a child continually breaks the rules of an activity and refuses to leave it), they will be assured of support. This partnership inhibits potentially volatile situations from occurring.

The PE teacher acts in a similar way, but also attends to organisational matters, such as equipment problems or making adjustments if a leader fails to turn up. This teamwork between the staff and the peer support leaders provides a network of proactive supervisors in the grounds.

CATERING FOR REPEAT OFFENDERS

Although a high percentage of the children take part quite happily in these lunchtime activities, some do not and a very small number of children continue to exhibit aggressive and antisocial behaviors. Consequently, a further step was taken to cater specifically for these repeat offenders.

Instead of continually applying the consequence of time-out inside, where repeat offenders do not have the opportunity to develop the important physical and social skills needed to be an effective contributor in the playground, the school employed a teacher aide to work with these children in the

The teacher aide program – developing catching skills with a rebound net

playground to coach them in developing a range of skills associated with football, netball and so on.

The teacher aide is required to collect nominated children from class, to supervise them during the program and then return them to line-up at the end of lunch. Participation in this program is non-negotiable for these children, and they are required to spend up to a full week on the program before they are permitted to have free access to other playground activities.

This arrangement has had at least three positive effects:

- the other children are safer in the playground

- activities run with little disruption

- the behavior of the children in the program improves, and as a consequence they are able to participate more effectively in other activities

AFTER-LUNCH ASSEMBLY

A child rings a bell at 1.15 pm to signal the end of lunchtime, and announces a reminder to all children to move to the line-up area. The children know that they must be at line-up within three minutes of the bell ringing. The line-up strategy was devised as a settling period to avoid problems which may occur in the transition from playground to the classroom. Each class is expected to be lined up and quiet at a central position on the sounding of the bell at 1.18 pm.

When the line-up was originally instigated, it was in itself a very difficult situation to control. However, through negotiation at class level with all students, a series of reward systems was set up. Classes are assigned points by the teacher on duty for lining up sensibly, and after each term the winning 'team' (the one with the most points) is given a previously negotiated reward, which may be, for example a special excursion or a barbecue lunch. This line-up time has gradually developed into a positive sharing time for all the school community. The change in children's behavior is exemplified by the following statements made recently by children:

'People were noisy; they used to bounce balls and fight each other.' (Kevin)

'Mrs Breheney used to have to ask people to be quiet all the time and sometimes some children would just keep talking anyway!'

(Matthew B.)

'It's better now because everyone is safe and you win prizes, and you can go to fun places as a reward.' (Michelle)

'We stand up straight now and don't talk. We share good things. We all like to win points and prizes.' (Matthew C.).

WHAT ABOUT WET WEATHER?

A special duty roster applies during wet lunchtimes. More teachers are required to be on duty, and senior staff add extra numbers. This proactive measure ensures a relaxed lunch hour for both students and teachers. Children know that classrooms are only for quiet activities such as reading, doing puzzles and playing board games, and are reminded of this before the lunch break. In order to ensure that there is likely to be something of interest to all children, a special wet-weather cupboard containing materials which children see and use only on wet days is maintained. Physical activity is available in an open plan area, although the peer support leaders have no formal role to play on wet days. Instead, the PE teacher is responsible for this, and in most instances a simple game of dodge ball is the most suitable, enabling a large number of children to play.

BENEFITS OF THE LUNCHTIME PROGRAM

The program has proved to have a number of significant benefits. There are fewer problems in the grounds. Peer support leaders are 'on the spot' and able to prevent many potential problems from developing further. Children develop skills in competitive situations, and are able to participate in quite intense sports such as football and basketball, without the games degenerating into a prolonged squabble, or something even worse.

The repetitive nature of the program ensures that children's skill levels definitely improve, and this leads to two important things: greater enjoyment and participation in the variety of physical activities and thus more attraction to the lunchtime program; and improved skill levels in children that possibly lead to life-long recreational opportunities.

The success of the program means that children have the opportunity to use a wider variety of equipment in the playground, since close supervision means that ropes, balls, bats and so on are less likely to be lost or stolen, or used as weapons.

Relationships between younger and older students have improved. With little previous contact between the two areas of the school, the junior primary children were very hesitant about approaching the older children to play, but now a large number of them do take part in the games with older children.

The peer support leaders have developed their leadership skills further. These c h i l d r e n already had these qualities to some d e g r e e before being selected as peer support leaders, but the skills have been enhanced over time and are frequently transferred to other aspects of their schooling.

Peer support – developing a notion of fairness and cooperation

Appropriate Behaviors in the Classroom program

As an adjunct to the whole-school Supportive Environment program, all teachers follow a behavior management program in their classroom in order to:

• create a positive classroom atmosphere

• promote cooperation and collaboration skills

• develop high self-esteem in all class members

• promote positive, appropriate behavior

A number of strategies are employed to create and maintain a positive classroom atmosphere which, in turn, fosters positive behavior and therefore provides opportunity for quality learning to occur. The intention is that children become responsible for their own behavior and, ultimately, for their own learning.

CLASSROOM ATMOSPHERE

Effective teachers create a community of learners with a positive attitude to learning. Critical to this is the strengthening of links between the curriculum as experienced and its perceived value to children in the present and in the future. A consequence of this is that children, parents and teachers become clearer about and more highly committed to the aims of education.

At Mayfield, a positive classroom atmosphere is established on the basis of mutual trust, respect, good relationships and support. Teachers take every opportunity to be positive with the children and display enthusiasm towards them and the tasks they are encountering. Comments which address the future, such as 'I've really been looking forward to this', and 'We're going to have a great day today' are commonplace. Similarly, though, the teacher needs to also reflect backwards with the children, and utterances such as 'What are the things that happened today to make it a great day?' ought be heard regularly.

TEAM-BUILDING

Successful team-building strategies, such as encouraging children to work regularly with a variety of peers rather than in friendship groups, are employed daily to foster and maintain positive relationships between all members of the class. Experiences involving the whole class as a team striving to achieve a common goal are planned for, and every child is encouraged to contribute to activities which will satisfy the common goal.

The teacher easily arrange simple games such as Beat the Clock, in which a group challenge such as 'See if you can build a 2-metre high tower out of 45 drinking straws in less than 10 minutes' is issued, and these generate a great deal of enthusiasm, excitement and suspense.

More complex and formal cooperative learning strategies are also used to good effect. A child or a pair of children 'specialising' in an aspect of a curriculum project, with the ultimate goal of contributing to a larger curriculum product which is the result of all students' efforts, is one example. Another strategy is to divide the class into heterogeneous teams so that members of each team work together and help each other to acquire curriculum knowledge in preparation for a quiz where students respond to questions to earn points for their team. These sorts of activities need to be an integral part of the curriculum, not an occasional appendage to it.

PROMOTING SELF-ESTEEM

Experiences which are designed specifically to help develop and maintain high self-esteem in children also occur on a daily basis. These may be introduced in a formal, overt way or in a more informal, personal and subtle manner. New and different ways are utilised continually to build and maintain positive self-images. Some useful strategies include:

The compliments ball game

- displaying 'Student of the Week' charts which detail positive comments about an individual
- using class compliment notes
- conducting class and individual point systems for curriculum and behavior purposes, with valued prizes being awarded periodically
- making a graffiti board available on which students are encouraged to write and draw positive comments about themselves and others in the class

Classroom management and organisation strategies

CLASS RULES

At Mayfield, high standards and expectations regarding behavior are set and clearly communicated to each child, and clear guidelines and rules relevant to all classroom behavior are established and learned, indeed over-learned.

The children and the teacher draw up a set of class rules at the beginning of the year and, of course, the children and teacher must understand and be committed to them. This is best achieved (surely can only be achieved) through a cooperative and collaborative process. So they can be referred to easily in future, the rules are categorised under key headings such as learning rules, communication rules, treatment (consequence) rules and safety rules.

The class rules are displayed prominently and attractively in the classroom and illustrated by the children as they feel appropriate. They are revisited constantly in a number of different ways such as by:

- focusing on a particular rule for a given week and encouraging the children to spot others following this rule, and following up by writing them a special note in recognition

- making revision of rules part of the language program

- having groups of children record the rules on video or audio tape followed by the class viewing or listening

- encouraging children to illustrate themselves or other children following the rules

- designing posters to promote the class rules

School rules are prominently displayed and are used as a focus for work undertaken in the classroom.

CLASSROOM MANAGEMENT

It is one thing to have a set of class rules, but it is quite another to have those rules at the absolute forefront in all matters relevant to the day-to-day activities of the classroom. The rules are seen as a tool rather than as a product, and, as a consequence, new rules emerge and others fade away. But their purpose is unwavering, and they are used consistently as an integral part of the classroom management repertoire. Teachers can refer to the rules as an agreement made between all members of the class, and utterances such as 'We have all agreed to follow our rules ...' and 'What does our rule say about that?' are commonplace.

The children need to know the rules very well and be able to articulate and explain them to the teacher, their peers and others. Of course, though, children will break the rules from time to time and this is when the teachers need to be ready and willing to enact a well-rehearsed sequence of responses. At Mayfield all teachers are trained in the following sequence:

1 Tactically ignore, unless the behavior is unsafe and is putting others in danger.

2 Restate the rule by asking: 'What is our communication rule about that?' and 'What should you be doing?'

3 If the inappropriate behavior continues, then the teacher may need to ensure that the child waits out the activity by sitting quietly away from the main focus of the activity with their back to the proceedings.

4 If the inappropriate behavior persists, or is putting others in danger or preventing them from learning, then the child may need to be removed by sending, via a reliable child, an exit card to the teacher next door who comes to collect rule breaker.

5 If the child refuses to go with the neighboring teacher or continues with the inappropriate behavior then senior staff assistance may be necessary to exit the child. It is the experience at Mayfield that this process is usually successful if used in moderation, and exiting a disruptive child from a class can have a very stabilising effect on the class in the short-term. Before the student is reintroduced to the class, it is important that conditions for future behavior are negotiated and agreed to.

6 Parents are called for discussion and counselling if necessary and, ultimately, suspension arrangements may have to be put in place.

A critical point in all of this is that these or similar steps must be agreed and practised in workshop settings by staff before any conflicts or problems occur. What is more, the process must be presented and discussed with the children so they are also aware of the steps that will occur. As a result, the children will be aware, in advance, of the consequences of any inappropriate behavior. (At the same time, of course, consequences of appropriate behaviors will be well known and believed by children as well.)

TEACHER SKILLS

Mayfield teachers use advice offered through school-based workshops, professional reading, attendance at seminars off-site and by research (such as that overviewed by Emmer and Evertson 1981) on successful management of classrooms. Behaviors such as the following are practised and refined continually.

- Teachers are very quick to recognise the source of any emerging inappropriate behavior by children and follow this with an equally prompt message of some sort, perhaps as overt as a fairly sharp verbal 'Stop that Johnny', or a more subtle raised eyebrow or a well-recognised cue such as a raised hand. A noise meter, which involves the teacher moving a pointer around a color-coded scale (for example blue = ideal noise level for the present activities, yellow = noise is getting a little too loud for the present activities, red = noise is unacceptable for the present activities) is a simple but effective way of controlling classroom noise.

- Teachers demonstrate a capacity to do several things at once. For example, while helping Omah with his work, the teacher continues to scan the room, raising an eyebrow to Joan, offering a frown to John and motioning Maria to come by her side. Through these sorts of actions the children recognise that the teacher has 'eyes in the back of her head'.

- Teachers practise keeping things moving along smoothly and at a good pace. While it is undesirable to exhort children continually to move ahead at a frenetic pace, it is equally undesirable to slow them down by having them wait unnecessarily for equipment to be brought out of cupboards, to have them sit with hand raised for long periods while the teacher devotes their time exclusively to someone or something, or by interrupting them regularly to give instructions which should have been given in a more organised manner prior to the activity starting. Good classroom managers plan for learning processes and content, but they also plan organisational matters such as the transitions from one activity to another.

- Teachers, even though their classroom may be organised largely to assist individuals and small groups to engage with their learning activities, also develop skills associated with alerting larger groups or the whole class to impending events.

- Teachers offer experiences to students which are judged to be of interest to them, which are likely to be seen as somewhat challenging but which offer a good chance of success, with the likelihood of valued and equitable rewards along the way and at the end.

- Teachers also ensure that the classroom is characterised by variety. This does not mean variety as in 'Children, last week we studied chapter 4 and learned the location, climate, landforms, soils and land use patterns of Chile. Now let's move to another part of the world. This week we'll study chapter 5 and learn the climate, landforms, soils and land **use** patters of Latvia.' One more fruitful way of catering for variety is, following Sergiovanni and Starratt's (1979) 'human curriculum', to organise learning experiences which focus from time to time on:

    students' **immediate concerns** (for example writing a story outline for a video they are about to see or a letter to a friend which focuses on the excitement of going to a carnival the day before)

    competencies they are likely to require in the **future** (such as researching the prerequisites an entrant into a chosen job may be expected to satisfy)

    knowledge which is **culturally defined** (such as identifying the world's longest river, highest mountain, largest city and so on)

    knowledge which is **personal** (for example, how it might feel to win a million dollars or climb the world's highest mountain)

individual endeavor (by which students work alone, perhaps in competition with peers)

cooperative activity (by which groups or the whole class work together toward a common goal)

The most enjoyable, memorable, productive and efficient learning experiences (for students and teacher alike) may be those which embody all six of the above aspects more or less simultaneously.

Other teachers will be more imaginative than us in devising such grand experiences, but the cross-country run is one that we have developed.The class, as a whole, draws up the broad outline for a cross-country running course. In smaller groups, students then stake out the course taking safety aspects into account, draw detailed maps, organise printing of the maps, and advertise a cross-country challenge in the school. As individuals, they seek sponsorship for running the course and then actually run the course. The class concludes the activity by donating the sponsorship money to a charity it has researched and selected.

CELEBRATION OF SUCCESS

The celebration of children's successes is very important as it acts as a powerful form of encouragement to the learner which, in turn, builds further academic and behavioral success in the future. Formal and highly public celebrations ought be a regular occurrence in all classrooms and the school generally, but less formal and public ones also have their place. Celebrations at Mayfield take the form of:

- presenting well-earned certificates at whole school assemblies

- displaying of children's work in the classroom and corridor

- presenting and discussing children's work at assemblies and in the outside community – especially through local newspaper supplements and regular newsletters which go home to parents

- presenting 'Student of the Week' awards

- sending notes home to parents ('I thought you'd like to know that Kim did excellent work in our language program today')

- distributing small prizes such as stickers, vouchers and edible treats appropriately

- maintaining a 'Top 8 Students' chart in the classroom
- inviting class applause at appropriate times
- offering personal positive oral and written comments
- organising whole-class trips and special treats

We are not reporting here that Mayfield is literally awash with satiated children – quite the reverse. Teachers and children negotiate the rewards, and they are valued and deserved by the children. Rebecca illustrates one example of this: Mackrill was driving her to McDonald's for a Big Mac as a negotiated consequence of her sustained appropriate behavior: 'Mrs Mackrill,' babbled Rebecca excitedly, 'this is like a dream come true for me. I have never been to McDonald's before.'

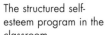

The structured self-esteem program in the classroom

CONFLICT RESOLUTION

Mayfield staff, as a consequence of their professional development activities, are able to ensure that their classrooms are fair and democratic places, in which conflicts are resolved positively and where children and teachers alike practise conflict resolution skills. Children are taught the skills of conflict resolution through the supportive environment and other programs in the school and are provided with opportunities to role-play and practise these skills in ad hoc and scheduled ways. Forums are convened in which children talk through and usually solve their problems whether they be of a classroom, playground or home nature. The class meeting is one such forum which proves successful.

CLASS MEETINGS

For a class meeting, the children are organised into a circle. Each child's class meeting card, with their name written on one side, is placed in front of them, face down. The leader of the meeting will ask those children with a problem to identify themselves by turning over their card so that their name is facing upwards. A number of children are likely to indicate that they have a problem, so each child, in turn, explains their problem in detail to the whole class. The other members the class listen and, by turning over their meeting card and waiting to be recognised by the leader of the meeting, ask questions to clarify details and pose possible solutions to the problem. The leader

A class meeting where all children are active participants in solving behavioral problems

of the meeting will ask the child with the focus problem to select one of the possible solutions that they believe may help to solve the problem and will be encouraged and coached where necessary to implement the solution as soon as possible.

At the beginning of the next class meeting, time is allotted for the children to provide feedback to the class group as to whether the solution worked satisfactorily for them. Sometimes other possible solutions need to be revisited by the group so the child can recall and implement one of the other suggestions if it is judged to be workable.

It is also important that the minutes of class meetings are recorded. The teacher may need to record them for younger children, but with older children, class members are rostered to record minutes while the meeting is in progress and to polish them after the meeting has finished.

SOCIAL SKILLS

Teachers discuss, model and teach social skills, and provide opportunities for children to acquire and practise these skills through role-play and other means. The children need to be given the opportunity to verbalise and go through the learning process kinesthetically so that these skills actually become part of their behavior repertoire rather than mere concepts about which they have some knowledge. Some important skills may be, for example, those concerned with saying 'please' and 'thankyou', with waiting for turns, with making friends, with joining in a game, and with behaving assertively.

Skills associated with cooperation are focused on frequently. Mayfield teachers do not assume that children understand what cooperation means and what it involves. The teacher asks questions such as 'What will we see when people are cooperating?' and 'What will it feel like when we work cooperatively?' The teachers organise opportunities for their children to observe group members cooperating (perhaps through watching a video) and engage children in brainstorming activities through which all the things involved in cooperation are identified. Contributions are likely to include: 'a group working together in their own space of the room without invading other groups' spaces'; 'people sitting in a circle listening to each other'; 'taking turns'; 'people concentrating on their own game'; 'students talking in quiet voices'; 'people having fair ways of working out who does what'; and 'people sharing resources, materials and ideas'.

Cooperative behaviors cannot be acquired easily in the classroom if the curriculum is exclusively competitive in nature. A competitive curriculum produces winners and losers in the classroom, and frequently some children are always winners while others are always losers. Cooperative learning experiences are planned across all areas of Mayfield's curriculum, and at the beginning of many cooperative activities the teachers ask 'What will I see when your group is cooperating?' Groups which cooperate well are identified and rewarded.

This is not to say that competition ought be eliminated from the classroom. Far from it. Nevertheless, it is possible to have wholesome competition and cooperation existing side by side. We spoke earlier of dividing the class into heterogeneous teams to work on learning tasks in preparation for a quiz or some other such closure, by which individual students earn points for their team. If the teams are heterogeneous in terms of demonstrated

Teaching cooperative skills in the classroom. 'What will I be doing when I am cooperating?'

ability in the main curriculum elements of the overall challenge (as well as being heterogeneous in terms of aspects such as ethnic background, age and gender), then the quiz can be organised so that 'A graders' compete against other 'A graders', and 'D graders' compete against other 'D graders' and so on for equal numbers of team points. This sort of competition is fair in that everyone has a reasonable chance of winning and, as such, can be highly motivating. Imagine young Mervyn, or Mary or Teresa, who have never received any accolades for academic success, being cheered on by team members as they come a gallant second behind Kate or Abdulla or Brian (who, similarly, have always been denied applause for academic achievement)! We have seen the pleasure young Mervyn, Kate and others have gained from performing well publicly at the level they are currently capable of.

COUNSELLING

Despite all that the teacher does to create a positive classroom atmosphere, conflicts and problems will still occur from time to time. In a supportive school such as Mayfield though, no one feels isolated and guidance is always available from other staff members to support the individual teacher.

A teacher spending time to counsel a child

When a problem or conflict does occur, counselling occurs immediately, or at least as soon as any cool-down period has elapsed. A counselling session involves the teacher and interested parties. The teacher leads discussion; however, the children resolve the conflict together and then decide on the consequences that may result because of their previous actions.

The skills learnt by their experiences in such counselling sessions ultimately equip children to solve many of their own problems, and, as time goes by, the teacher may not even need to be party to discussions between students who are attempting to resolve differences themselves, but may simply keep a watchful eye on the proceedings.

TIME-OUT

At Mayfield Primary School, the time-out space is a designated semi-enclosed area near the principal's office where children are sent at recess or lunch as a possible consequence of their negative behavior. Each day, teachers are rostered exclusively onto the area during their duty time. Use of time-out is documented with dates, names and reasons for such a consequence, and the documentation informs any future discussions with children or their parents. Senior staff monitor the time-out area regularly to support the rostered duty teacher, as it can become troublesome if there are too many children or if there is a collection of volatile personalities.

During time-out it is expected that children do not communicate with each other or with the supervising teacher. Time is allocated for children to eat their lunch and to go to the toilet, but otherwise it is regarded as a time for quiet reflection and isolation from others.

SOME IMPORTANT CONSIDERATIONS

Time-out is a behavior management option that requires careful thought. It is important that it is not used for minor misdemeanors but for serious threats to safety of others or constant abuse or disruption. Time-out is viewed as a consequence of behavior, but it is judged by staff that long sessions or extended periods of time spent in time-out are not effective, and that it is far better to engage children in a more productive program of intervention such as the teacher aide program at lunchtime where they can be learning positive interaction and cooperative skills.

COOL-OFF SEAT

As in most schools, there is a designated seat in Mayfield's playground for minor behavioral infringements. Children can be asked to use this area, known to all as the 'blue seat', if they have been exhibiting inappropriate behavior while playing outside, but, again, this consequence is selected to enable them to reflect on their behavior and to help to diffuse a potentially troublesome situation before any serious conflict occurs.

MATCHING CONSEQUENCES TO THE BEHAVIOR

The position taken by Mayfield staff is that it is important to match a specific consequence to a specific behavior if at all possible. They therefore limit the use of time-out, which will usually be seen by students as a 'generalist' or 'umbrella' consequence. It is felt that too often in schools, consequences that are not purposeful are meted out to children with the result that they feel more stressed and angry. It is preferable for children to be engaged in some productive experience, for example working with a younger child under supervision, where they can learn not to perform the inappropriate behavior and where they can develop socially acceptable ways of going about their lives.

If one maxim can sum up Mayfield's attitude toward consequences of inappropriate behavior it is that 'The certainty and matching of a consequence is important, not its severity'. For example, if a child has been throwing stones in the playground the consequence may be to walk with a duty teacher and collect and dispose of stones from the playground; or if he has defaced school property in some way, he may work at remedying the damage; or if she has destroyed property she might work during her own time doing 'jobs' around the school to 'earn funds' to pay for repairs or a replacement; or if he or she has been bullying some younger or smaller children, it could be appropriate to involve him or her in some game or activity during the lunch hour to help build positive relationships between the bully and the bullied and perhaps some nominated friends.

The Behavior Recovery program

Mayfield Primary has adopted a Behavior Recovery program based on Bill Rogers' concepts, and it is integral to the school's functioning. Behavior recovery is an intensive behavior modification program carried out between a teacher and an individual child. It has two specific purposes:

- to develop an awareness within the child of the inappropriateness of a specific behavior
- to have students over-learn positive strategies to enable the particular behavior to become more acceptable

The focus child is always one whose behavior is of serious concern, and the program requires that the teacher be committed to assisting the child to 'get it right'. A senior staff member or another supporting teacher assists by enabling the teacher engaging with the focus child to be released from other activities for a short period of time each day for the duration of the program.

THE PROCESS OF BEHAVIOR RECOVERY

It is essential that the child has a clear understanding of what specifically it is that he or she is doing or not doing that is causing the teacher and other class members such great concern. One of the most powerful strategies for helping a child to identify a specific behavior is to model that behavior back to them. This process requires the teacher to withdraw a child from the class, and to actually demonstrate the behavior. For example, say the behavior is continual calling out or otherwise disrupting the class during whole-class teaching time. The child sits down while the teacher demonstrate what it looks like when someone jumps up and calls out loudly.

It can be quite difficult for a teacher to act like a child at times, but it can also be very effective. Previously prepared drawings can also give the child a graphic image of the behavior. 'This is what it looks like when you are disrupting the class. Can you see yourself in the drawing?' A second drawing will depict 'This is how the class looks when you are not disrupting their activities'. It is important that only one behavior is targeted at a time

Once the behavior has been identified, the teacher and the child must meet each day, usually just before a scheduled break, to discuss progress made in achieving the appropriate behavior. Any difficulties are identified, options that could have been taken are discussed, and strategies that can be used in the future are agreed upon.

As with any behavior modification program, focusing on and celebrating positive behaviors is essential, and in the Behavior Recovery program some kind of record of progress, a chart or similar document say, is maintained to act as a reinforcer for the child and to focus discussion with parents.

Inevitably, problems will occur in a classroom or in the playground. Following are some scenarios and suggested actions a teacher can implement as a result of such situations.

A CHILD SWEARS AT ANOTHER CHILD IN THE CLASSROOM

Tell the child who was sworn at that '... you need to remind Amelia of the school rule in relation to swearing and also, you need to tell Amelia that you don't like it when you are sworn at.' This helps the child with shared ownership of the problem, and with asserting their rights, while sending a message that you are supporting the rules of the school.

A CHILD SWEARS AT YOU

Firstly, remain calm and don't be offended. The swearing is the secondary problem and you need to establish what the real problem is first.

Remind the child of the rule: 'What's the rule about swearing Phillip?' Then later, after you finish what you are doing, calmly go over to him and establish what the problem is. 'You seem to be upset today. What is the problem?'

A CHILD IS OPENLY DEFIANT OR REFUSES TO FOLLOW AN INSTRUCTION

Again, remain calm and give them a choice: 'You can join in with this work now, or you can do it during lunchtime. You make the choice.' If they choose the lunchtime option, then ensure that an arrangement is made so that this can happen, e.g. you might have to change a duty, or ask senior staff to supervise. Remember, that it is the certainty of the consequence that is important, not the severity.

If a child continues to be disruptive or defiant, and is causing you and the other children in the class an amount of stress, exiting the child from the classroom to give everyone some relief is always an option.

OTHER TIPS ...

Don't argue and don't enter into a power struggle.

'There's a rule for that, let's use it thanks!'

DOB (Don't obey bullies) (Bill Rogers)

Turn away immediately to indicate trust and a high expectation that it will happen without supervision.

Establish the 3 Rs – rules, rights and responsibilities – and always work from them.

Avoid unnecessary conflict – arguing, demanding.

Start a new day a-fresh – don't drag up old problems.

Develop consistent follow-up.

The Life-skills program

The Life-skills program is for children who have been identified as needing additional help to enable them to function adequately within a community.

A small number of children (seven or eight at a time) are selected by staff to work for one afternoon per week with a teacher aide to develop basic skills such as those involved in cooking and simple crafts, general hygiene and health, letter-writing, accessing information from the community, shopping at the supermarket and managing a budget carefully. Each round of the program lasts for up to 10 weeks and is coordinated by a teacher or senior staff member.

Recently the program has changed part of its focus slightly, and groups now also engage in profit-making enterprise projects such as making morning tea and selling it to the staff.

The Human Relationships program

Mayfield staff recognise that some children display inappropriate behaviors in regard to human relationships – particularly their treatment of girls and women and in the way they talk about human reproduction.

Their partial solution to this problem is to employ, out of the school's funds, a specially trained nurse to work in classes alongside teachers from K to 6 on a program which focuses on human sexuality and relationships within families. In total, the nurse spends about 50 hours at the school in a block during second term, which means that all children in the school are involved directly for about four sessions of 20 minutes each.

This program was funded initially as a consequence of a submission to a Priority Projects Scheme, but in recent years it has been agreed that the need for such a program is so great that it has been funded from the school's normal resource package.

The trained nurse also conducts, at school, a parent program of about one hour in duration before the classroom sessions begin to ensure that parents have a firm understanding of the program's aims and content.

JUNIOR PRIMARY SESSIONS (K–2)

The program's content for the younger children includes

discussion about the family and focuses on the child as a part of a family unit. The children are encouraged to find out as much as they can from their mother about their birth, what the day was like, what time it was, who was there and so on. The program also focuses on the similarities and differences between boys and girls.

SENIOR PRIMARY SESSIONS (3–6)

The sessions for the older children are based on similar topics to K–2 sessions, but include greater detail on relationships. The information is appropriate to the children's level of development and their needs and interests.

The Technology program

The Technology program is run in a workshop which was once a groundsman's store. This program was initiated by a social worker who was based at the local secondary school but who had responsibilities within Mayfield. The social worker developed the program so that he could begin to cement positive relationships between himself and a small group of children with whom he felt he may be having considerable contact when they reached secondary school.

Children selected to work with the social worker on this program are some of those from years 5 and 6 who are having social or behavioral difficulties in the classroom or playground setting.

The aims of the program are to:
- provide children with an opportunity to engage in positive contact with an adult outside the classroom
  - facilitate their development of cooperation and communication skills with peers

The apprentice and craftsman working together

- assist with the development of a positive self-image

- engage them in problem-solving and technological skills

The major strategy used to satisfy these aims is the provision of a brief to groups of children who then have to design, make and appraise a particular product, such as a model aeroplane.

The Philosophy for Children program

Mackrill introduced the Philosophy for Children program as part of the classroom support role she performed as senior teacher in the school. Many of the aims of the Philosophy for Children program, developed originally in the United States by Matthew Lipman, are mutually compatible with and reinforcing of the aims of the Supportive School Environment program.

Philosophy for Children provides a basis for children to engage in dialogue within a 'community of inquiry'. During each session, children are encouraged to talk about their own ideas and to listen, in a supportive way, to the views of others. The stimulus for such discussion comes from a series of specially written stories which are full of intriguing ideas and concepts with a strong base in the area of philosophy. Recently, other material (De Haan, MacColl & McCutcheon 1995) has been published in Australia using picture books as a basis for philosophical dialogue.

The program is conducted by a senior teacher for all children across the school. Sessions normally last about 30 minutes and are scheduled in children's normal classrooms. The program has three important features. Firstly, it provides children with experiences to develop thinking and reasoning skills such as reflecting, listening, making connections, presenting and supporting arguments, detecting fallacies in arguments, appreciating the views of others, questioning, describing, expressing thoughts and ideas, and cooperating.

Secondly, the content of the program is the same content which has occupied the minds of thinkers for centuries. Topics include the notion of fairness, the nature of knowledge, exploration of self, moral issues, truth and goodness. It is judged that these skills and concepts can be transferred from one situation to another, including situations where conflict and inappropriate behaviors are latent or manifest.

The third important feature of the program is the development of a community of inquiry. Within such a community, all participants are encouraged to contribute to discussion and dialogue without fear of denigration. Comment is encouraged by all members of the community, and is treated with respect and sensitivity. Both the ethos of the program and the strategies employed within the community of inquiry match particularly well with the Supportive School Environment program at Mayfield.

Coda

We have presented a range of programs and actions which have been germane to Mayfield's success in limiting violence and promoting positive behaviors within the school. The essential keys, though, are rather less tangible, and the central one, we feel, is an attitude of 'We are going to get this right, and we are going to nag and nibble at the problem and support each other in doing so until we do get it right.'

Six Cs' seem to sum up our experience best:

- concern for good relationships
- commitment to getting it right
- cohesion among staff members
- collaboration among all stakeholders
- coping through action
- celebrating success whenever and wherever it occurs

Mayfield Primary School's people move forward to the future with considerable satisfaction. Much has been done to make the school into a place in which good teaching and learning occurs. Nevertheless, while this state of affairs is quite robust it cannot be taken for granted. The future demands that the 'Six Cs' be nurtured carefully and consciously, and when the people of Mayfield say, 'It's all too hard,' they would be well advised to think of what it would be like if the coin were allowed to flip over to reveal its dark side again.

References and further reading

Argyris, C. & Schon, D. A. 1978, *Organizational Learning: A Theory of Action Perspective*, Addison-Wesley, Reading Mass.

Balson, M. 1987, *Understanding Classroom Behaviour*, Australian Council for Educational Research, Melbourne. (1987, State Mutual Book & Periodical Service Ltd, New York.)

Banks, D. 1992, 'Keys to school effectiveness' in *Making Schools More Effective*, B. McGaw, K. Piper, D. Banks & B. Evans, Australian Council for Educational Research, Melbourne.

Banks, D. 1994, Redefining effectiveness to meet new imperatives for schooling: Some ideas looking for a framework, Paper read at the International Congress on School Effectiveness and Improvement, Melbourne, January.

Boulding, K. E. 1956, *The Image*, University of Michigan Press, Ann Arbor.

Caldwell, B. & Spinks, J. 1986, *Policy-Making and Planning for School Effectiveness*, Tasmanian Education Department, Hobart.

Chapman, J. 1993, 'Leadership, management and "the effectiveness of schooling": A response to Mr Gradgrind', *Journal of Educational Administration*, vol. 31, no. 4 pp. 4–18.

Dalton, J. & Collis, M. 1990, *Becoming Responsible Learners: Strategies for Positive Classroom Management*, rev. edn, Eleanor Curtain Publishing, Melbourne. (1990, Heinemann, Portsmouth, NH.)

De Haan, C., MacColl, S. & McCuthcheon, L. 1995, *Philosophy with Kids*, Longman, Melbourne.

Emmer, E. T. & Evertson, C. M. 1981, 'Synthesis of research on classroom management', *Educational Leadership*, January,

Grady, N. B. 1993, 'Examining teachers' images through metaphor', *Studies in Educational Administration*, no. 58, pp. 23–31.

Grose, M. 1994, *Fair Go: A Practical Guide to Managing Children*, Phoenix Education, Melbourne.

Holdoway, E. A. & Johnson, N. A. 1993, 'School effectiveness and effectiveness indicators', *School Effectiveness and School Improvement*, vol. 4, no. 3, pp. 165–88.

Hoy, W. K. & Miskel, C. G. 1987, *Educational Administration: Theory Research and Practice*, Random House, New York.

Johnson, D. W. & Johnson, R. T. 1989, *Leading the Cooperative School*, Interaction Book Co., Edina, Minnesota.

Kilmann, R. H., Saxton, M. J., Serpa and Associates (eds) 1985, *Gaining Control of the Corporate Culture*, Jossey-Bass, San Francisco.

Miles, M. B. 1987, Practical guidelines for school administrators: How to get there, Paper read at the Symposium on Effective Schools Programs and the Urban High School: The Management of Large-Scale Change, American Educational Research Association Meeting, Washington DC, April.

Morgan, G. 1983, 'Research as engagement: A personal view' in *Beyond Method: Strategies for Social Research*, ed. G. Morgan, Sage, Thousand Oaks, CA.

Morgan, G. 1986, *Images of Organization*, Sage, Thousand Oaks, CA.

Mulford, B. 1986, *Indicators of School Effectiveness: A Practical Approach*, Australian Council for Educational Administration, Melbourne.

Peterson, L. & Gannoni, A. 1992, *Stop Think Do*, Australian Council for Educational Research, Melbourne.

Purkey, C. & Smith, M. 1983, 'Effective schools: A review', *Elementary School Journal*, vol. 18, pp. 427–52.

Reid, K., Hopkins, D. & Holly, P. 1987, *Towards the Effective School: The Problems and Some Solutions*, Blackwell, Oxford.

Rogers, B. 1990, *You Know the Fair Rule*, Australian Council for Educational Research, Melbourne. (1990, State Mutual Book & Periodical Service Ltd, New York.)

Rogers, B. 1995, *Behaviour Management: A Whole School Approach*, Ashton Scholastic, Gosford, NSW.

Sergiovanni, T. J. 1991, *The Principalship: A Reflective Practice Perspective*, 2nd edn, Allyn and Bacon, Boston.

Sergiovanni, T. J. & Starratt, R. J. 1979, *Supervision: Human Perspectives*, McGraw-Hill, New York.

Sheive, L. T. & Schoenheit, M. B. 1987, 'Vision and the work life of educational leaders' in *Leadership: Examining the Elusive, Yearbook of the Association for Supervision and Curriculum Development*, eds L. T. Sheive, & M. B. Schoenheit, ASCA, Alexandria, Virginia.

Slavin, R., Schlomo, S., Kagan, S., Lazarowitz, W & Schmuck, R., 1985, *Learning to Co-operate, Co-operating to Learn*, Plenum Press, New York.

Stevens, R. J. & Slavin, R. E., 1995, 'The cooperative elementary school: Effects on students' achievement, attitudes, and social relations', *American Educational Research Journal*, Summer, vol. 32, no. 2, pp. 321–51.

Tasmanian Early Childhood Senior Staff Association – Northern Branch, 1986, *A Study into the Incidence of Children with Behaviour Difficulties: K-3*, Education Department of Tasmania, Hobart.

Wilks, S. 1995, *Critical and Creative Thinking: Strategies for Classroom Inquiry*, Eleanor Curtain Publishing, Melbourne. (1995, Heinemann, Portsmouth, NH.)

Index

Other titles by Australian authors

Becoming Responsible Learners:
Strategies for positive classroom management
Joan Dalton and Mark Collis

An extremely practical and highly readable book on strategies and guidelines for classroom management, this best-selling book is the result of observing effective collaborative teachers at work and talking to them about their beliefs and classroom practices. *Becoming Responsible Learners* is an invaluable asset to teachers who want to encourage children to take responsibility for their own learning and behavior.
ISBN 0 435 08568 9 illustrated 80 pp

The Collaborative Classroom:
A guide to co-operative learning
Susan and Tim Hill

The Collaborative Classroom is a creative and practical guide for teachers who want to implement and gain maximum benefit for students from co-operative learning. The book focuses and identifies the areas where co-operative skills are needed: forming groups and managing differences. *The Collaborative Classroom* is both practical and encouraging and includes dozens of activities to get the beginning teacher started.
ISBN 0 435 08525 5 illustrated 162 pp

Critical and Creative Thinking
Strategies for classroom inquiry
Susan Wilks

Better questioning, greater participation and more open discussion lead to a positive change in classroom dynamics, creating an environment in which children learn to value independent and autonomous thinking.

   Critical and Creative Thinking provides teaching strategies to develop and refine thinking skills and processes such as: identifying assumptions; prioritis-
ing; seeking alternatives; speculating; drawing inferences; identifying faulty logic.
ISBN 0 435 08869 6 illustrated 128 pp

Thinking for Themselves:
Developing strategies for reflective learning
Jeni Wilson and Lesley Wing Jan

By encouraging children to think about their learning and to become aware of and control their thinking processes, teachers can help them to become active, responsible learners - learners who can make their own decisions, choose appropriate strategies, assess their own work and set their own goals. *Thinking for Themselves* provides activities for the development of skills and strategies within a range of existing programs and starting points and ideas to help the implementation of reflective teaching and learning programs.

   Contents include: getting started; developing the appropriate learning environment; program planning; negotiating with students; questioning and self-assessment techniques.
ISBN 0 435 08805 X illustrated 124 pp

I Teach:
A guide to inspiring classroom leadership
Joan Dalton and Julie Boyd

Specific and practical insights into the 'what' and 'how' of effective learning and teaching presented succinctly and visually.

   Contents include: identify your goals; walk the leader's walk; build relationships with others; create a community of learners; empower growth in others; work on self- growth - identify personal strengths, highlight areas for self-improvement and plan for balanced leadership.
ISBN 0 435 08782 7   illustrated 128 pp

Integrating Socially
Planning integrated units of work for social education
Julie Hamston and Kath Murdoch

Integrating Socially is essentially a book about classroom practise. It provides a comprehensive and practical guide to developing integrated units of work for social education, incorporating a focus on language. It includes seven planned units on topics covering a broad spectrum of social education which serve as a resource for teaching and also act as models for teachers' own planning. The units have been designed to engage teachers and learners in shared investigations - developing critical understandings about the social world is seen as a shared enterprise between teacher and learner.

The book provides an overview of the theory that guides the practise, outlines the kind of content that should be covered in a comprehensive social education curriculum and provides information on how the units can be adapted to meet particular needs. Useful strategies for social education and different ways of learning which can be used in many different aspects of the school curriculum are outlined. Explicit assistance in planning integrated units of work for social education is provided.
ISBN 0 435 08899 8   172 pp

The Big Picture:
Integrating students' learning
Edited by Marilyn Woolley and Keith Pigdon

The Big Picture addresses the key issues which are central to the idea of the integrated curriculum and translates them into practical classroom advice.

Contents include: context and framework - the ideas which drive teachers' curriculum planning; a planning model: bringing the components together in an organised yet flexible structure; the model in practise - activities and strategies; language and the integrated curriculum; integrated learning and specific curriculum practice; assessment and evaluation: for the learner, the teacher and the community; whole school change - it starts in your classroom.
ISBN 0 435 08792 4 illustrated 128 pp

One Teacher's Classroom:
Strategies for successful teaching and learning
Dale Gordon

Within the context of whole language learning, this is record of the successful strategies of an experienced, competent and dedicated teacher who has built up a framework of teaching practice. The book provides models, guidelines and strategies to support these aims.

Contents include: creating a learning environment - providing time, providing a place, providing resources; making learning easier for learners - integrating the conditions for learning, providing real reasons to learn, demonstrating learning; allowing learners to function at their full potential - taking responsibility, approximation, expectations for learning; finding out about learning - feedback, assessment and reporting.
ISBN 1 875327 15 0 illustrated 128 pp

The Literacy Agenda:
Issues for the nineties
Elaine Furniss and Pamela Green, Editors

A book to provoke, encourage and inspire you to 'have a go' at confronting the key issues of literacy development in your own classroom. Each chapter is a collaboration between a leading teacher educator and a classroom teacher, so that the practical implications of the issues are always addressed.

Contents include: how children learn to read; what happens if they don't succeed; equal opportunities for girls and boys; how to use the literacy cultures that children bring to the classroom; the sort of talk that takes place in classrooms; assessment procedures; second language learners; how to involve parents.
ISBN 0 435 08707 X   illustrated   178 pp

Literacy Evaluation:
Issues and practicalities
Christine Bouffler, Editor

The increasing pressure for greater accountability has put assessment high on the educational agenda. There are four major groups requiring performance information: students, teachers, parents and educational systems. *Literacy Evaluation* surveys some of the recent developments in language assessment - in

the United States, the United Kingdom and in
Australia - which attempt to satisfy the needs of
these groups.
ISBN   0 345 08791 6   120 pp

Teach On:
Teaching strategies for reading and writing work-shops
David Hornsby, Jo-Ann Parry and Deborah Sukarna

Teach On recognises the importance of two things:
first, that for effective learning to occur, teachers
must 'tune in' to children's strengths and needs; second, that they must teach! This practical book outlines several strategies and procedures that have
been successful in classrooms where whole language philosophy guides the teacher's program.
ISBN   0 453 08790 8   84 pp

Each of these titles is published by Heinemann